T0321856

Crowdsourcing and Probabilistic Decision-Making in Software Engineering:

Emerging Research and Opportunities

Varun Gupta
University of Beira Interior, Covilha, Portugal

A volume in the Advances in
Systems Analysis, Software
Engineering, and High Performance
Computing (ASASEHPC) Book Series

Published in the United States of America by
 IGI Global
 Engineering Science Reference (an imprint of IGI Global)
 701 E. Chocolate Avenue
 Hershey PA, USA 17033
 Tel: 717-533-8845
 Fax: 717-533-8661
 E-mail: cust@igi-global.com
 Web site: http://www.igi-global.com

Library of Congress Cataloging-in-Publication Data

Names: Gupta, Varun, 1987- author.
Title: Crowdsourcing and probabilistic decision-making in software
 engineering : emerging research and opportunities / Varun Gupta, editor.
Description: Hershey, PA : Engineering Science Reference, [2019] | Includes
 bibliographical references.
Identifiers: LCCN 2019005480| ISBN 9781522596592 (h/c) | ISBN 9781522596608
 (s/c) | ISBN 9781522596615 (eISBN)
Subjects: LCSH: Crowdsourcing. | Statistical decision. | Software engineering.
Classification: LCC QA76.9.H84 G87 2019 | DDC 005.1--dc23 LC record available at https://lccn.
loc.gov/2019005480

This book is published in the IGI Global book series Advances in Systems Analysis, Software Engineering, and High Performance Computing (ASASEHPC) (ISSN: 2327-3453; eISSN: 2327-3461)

British Cataloguing in Publication Data
A Cataloguing in Publication record for this book is available from the British Library.

For electronic access to this publication, please contact: eresources@igi-global.com.

Advances in Systems Analysis, Software Engineering, and High Performance Computing (ASASEHPC) Book Series

Vijayan Sugumaran
Oakland University, USA

ISSN:2327-3453
EISSN:2327-3461

MISSION

The theory and practice of computing applications and distributed systems has emerged as one of the key areas of research driving innovations in business, engineering, and science. The fields of software engineering, systems analysis, and high performance computing offer a wide range of applications and solutions in solving computational problems for any modern organization.

The **Advances in Systems Analysis, Software Engineering, and High Performance Computing (ASASEHPC) Book Series** brings together research in the areas of distributed computing, systems and software engineering, high performance computing, and service science. This collection of publications is useful for academics, researchers, and practitioners seeking the latest practices and knowledge in this field.

COVERAGE

- Metadata and Semantic Web
- Enterprise Information Systems
- Storage Systems
- Performance Modelling
- Computer System Analysis
- Engineering Environments
- Virtual Data Systems
- Software Engineering
- Computer Graphics
- Human-Computer Interaction

IGI Global is currently accepting manuscripts for publication within this series. To submit a proposal for a volume in this series, please contact our Acquisition Editors at Acquisitions@igi-global.com or visit: http://www.igi-global.com/publish/.

Titles in this Series

For a list of additional titles in this series, please visit:
https://www.igi-global.com/book-series/advances-systems-analysis-software-engineering/73689

Metrics and Models for Evaluating the Quality and Effectiveness of ERP Software
Geoffrey Muchiri Muketha (Murang'a University of Technology, Kenya) and Elyjoy Muthoni
Micheni (Technical University of Kenya, Kenya)
Engineering Science Reference • © 2020 • 391pp • H/C (ISBN: 9781522576785) • US
$225.00 (our price)

*User-Centered Software Development for the Blind and Visually Impaired Emerging
Research and Opportunities*
Teresita de Jesús Álvarez Robles (Universidad Veracruzana, Mexico) Francisco Javier Álvarez
Rodríguez (Universidad Autónoma de Aguascalientes, Mexico) and Edgard Benítez-Guerrero
(Universidad Veracruzana, Mexico)
Engineering Science Reference • © 2020 • 173pp • H/C (ISBN: 9781522585398) • US
$195.00 (our price)

Architectures and Frameworks for Developing and Applying Blockchain Technology
Nansi Shi (Logic International Consultants, Singapore)
Engineering Science Reference • © 2019 • 337pp • H/C (ISBN: 9781522592570) • US
$245.00 (our price)

Human Factors in Global Software Engineering
Mobashar Rehman (Universiti Tunku Abdul Rahman, Malaysia) Aamir Amin (Universiti
Tunku Abdul Rahman, Malaysia) Abdul Rehman Gilal (Sukkur IBA University, Pakistan)
and Manzoor Ahmed Hashmani (University Technology PETRONAS, Malaysia)
Engineering Science Reference • © 2019 • 381pp • H/C (ISBN: 9781522594482) • US
$245.00 (our price)

Interdisciplinary Approaches to Information Systems and Software Engineering
Alok Bhushan Mukherjee (North-Eastern Hill University Shillong, India) and Akhouri
Pramod Krishna (Birla Institute of Technology Mesra, India)
Engineering Science Reference • © 2019 • 299pp • H/C (ISBN: 9781522577843) • US
$215.00 (our price)

701 East Chocolate Avenue, Hershey, PA 17033, USA
Tel: 717-533-8845 x100 • Fax: 717-533-8661
E-Mail: cust@igi-global.com • www.igi-global.com

Table of Contents

Foreword viii

Preface x

Acknowledgment xiv

Chapter 1
Markov Decision Theory-Based Crowdsourcing Software Process Model 1
    Kamalendu Pal, City, University of London, UK

Chapter 2
I-Way: A Cloud-Based Recommendation System for Software Requirement
Reusability 23
    Chetna Gupta, Jaypee Institute of Information Technology, Noida, India
    Surbhi Singhal, Jaypee Institute of Information Technology, Noida,
        India
    Astha Kumari, Jaypee Institute of Information Technology, Noida, India

Chapter 3
Requirement-Based Test Approach and Traceability for High-Integrity
Airborne Embedded Systems 35
    Sudha Srinivasan, Aeronautical Development Agency (ADA), Bangalore,
        India
    D. S. Chauhan, GLA University Mathura, Mathura, India

Chapter 4
A Systematic Literature Review on Risk Assessment and Mitigation
Approaches in Requirement Engineering 51
    Priyanka Chandani, Jaypee Institute of Information Technology, Noida,
        India
    Chetna Gupta, Jaypee Institute of Information Technology, Noida, India

Chapter 5
Agile Team Measurement to Review the Performance in Global Software
Development 81
    Chamundeswari Arumugam, SSN College of Engineering, India
    Srinivasan Vaidyanathan, Cognizant Technology Solutions, India

Chapter 6
Improving Construction Management Through Advanced Computing and
Decision Making 94
    Varun Gupta, University of Beira Interior, Covilha, Portugal
    Aditya Raj Gupta, Amity University, Noida, India
    Utkarsh Agrawal, Amity University, Noida, India
    Ambika Kumar, Amity University, Noida, India
    Rahul Verma, Amity University, Noida, India

Chapter 7
An Investigation on Quality Perspective of Software Functional Artifacts 109
    Vimaladevi M., Pondicherry Engineering College, Puducherry, India
    Zayaraz G., Pondicherry Engineering College, Puducherry, India

Chapter 8
An Analysis of UI/UX Designing With Software Prototyping Tools 134
    Shruti Gupta, Amity University, Delhi, India

Chapter 9
Improving Financial Estimation in Construction Management Through
Advanced Computing and Decision Making 146
    Varun Gupta, University of Beira Interior, Covilha, Portugal
    Aditya Raj Gupta, Amity University, Noida, India
    Utkarsh Agrawal, Amity University, Noida, India
    Ambika Kumar, Amity University, Noida, India
    Rahul Verma, Amity University, Noida, India

Chapter 10
Independent Verification and Validation of FPGA-Based Design for Airborne
Electronic Applications...153
 Sudha Srinivasan, Aeronautical Development Agency (ADA), Bangalore,
  India
 D. S. Chauhan, GLA University, Mathura, India
 Rekha R., Aeronautical Development Agency (ADA), Bangalore, India

Related Readings.. 167

About the Contributors 177

Index.. 181

Foreword

If the experience of the last few decades of Software Engineering is anything to go by, we seem to always be catching up with the innovations taking place in a hyperactive market, increasing the chances of developing systems that don't fully take account of the needs of users, don't meet legal obligations and end up compromising reliability, security and maintainability.

Fortunately, the software industry is good at learning as we go. Each innovation is typically followed by excitement in the market, some unfortunate system failures due to oversight in the requirements and, most importantly, a realisation that our Software Engineering methods need to adapt to meet the new demands. Examples of this learning process include an era where formal methods of software engineering were developed in the 90's to meet the need to ensure reliability in safety critical applications, and more recently, the drive to adopt agile development methods to increase productivity and reduce risks.

The most recent efforts to improve the software engineering process, which is the subject of this edited collection, is to utilise crowdsourcing and methods from machine learning. Although crowdsourcing, which was advocated by Jeff Howe as a way of achieving "wisdom of the crowd" as far back as 2006, its proposed use for developing software has been more recent and is growing rapidly. The essence of crowdsourcing for software development is to utilise a community of external stakeholders, including potential users, analysts and programmers, to participate in the development of an application on the premise that all stakeholders will eventually gain mutual benefits.

This broad view of crowdsourcing and use of machine learning for software engineering raises many questions, such as:

- How does one use crowdsourcing effectively in the different phases of software development, from requirements elicitation to testing and then maintenance and deployment?
- We know from recent history, that new software engineering methodologies are not universally applicable, so are there specific types of applications where use of crowdsourcing and use of machine learning is best?

This edited collection brings together several studies addressing such questions. The chapters include systematic reviews of the field, case studies showing the use of machine learning and crowdsourcing in domains such as construction and aerospace, and key perspectives from the IT industry.

The chapters in this book will provide valuable insight for both academics pursuing research in this field and software development companies, who are seeking to improve their processes by using crowdsourcing or AI methods for software engineering.

Sunil Vadera
University of Salford, UK
July 2019

Preface

AN OVERVIEW

Software Engineering deals with the delivery of high quality software to its users within time and budgets. The development is done by software development organization either as bespoke or as mass market product. There are variety of tools and techniques that software engineers can use to achieve the objectives of high quality software. Different techniques provides different opportunities of improvements. Improvement in this area will improve the quality of delivered software that will impact positively the domains where the software has to function. The evolution of the software makes the different activities more challenging. The challenges are further amplified because these days the inputs are taken from crowds as the software will be used by these crowds only. The various solutions of various problems faced in development of the software either co-located or distributed for single customer of for mass markets, must be capable of handling the crowds in efficient manner. This requires integration of various areas like Artificial Intelligence especially Natural Language Processing, Big Data, data mining etc to improve the software engineering. The decision making involved in software development is based on probabilistic reasoning as the complete process is uncertain and hence the probabilistic decision models finds its role in overall improvements in crowd based software engineering.

This book provides relevant theoretical frameworks and the latest empirical research findings in the broad area of software engineering. The research contained in this book highlights issues, challenges, techniques and practices relevant to software engineering in general and crowd sourcing in particular. The research addressing software engineering in general provides researchers the knowledge about constraints and best practices applicable for crowd soured software engineering.

TARGET AUDIENCE

The research findings contained in this book is ideal for the software engineers who want to improve the manner the software is developed by increasing the accuracy of probabilistic reasoning supporting their decision making and getting automation support. It will also provide them with the latest solution strategies for various problems faced during development and various best practices through case studies. This book is ideal for professionals and researchers working in the field of software engineering for bespoke and mass market developments. Moreover, the book provides insights and support software engineers and higher management executives with the latest effective solutions, automation supports and case studies about software engineering issues, challenges, techniques and practices.

ORGANISATION OF BOOK

This book is organised into ten chapters. Each chapter provides insight into software engineering related aspects. Chapter 1 analyses the process of software development at a crowdsourced platform. The work analyses and identifies the phase wise deliverables in a competitive software development problem. It also proposes the use of Markov Decision Theory to model the dynamics of the development processes of a software by using a simulated example. Chapter 2 addresses the problem of effectively searching and selecting relevant requirements for reuse meeting stakeholders objectives through knowledge discovery and data mining techniques maintained over a cloud platform. Knowledge extraction of similar requirement(s) is performed on data and meta-data stored in central repository using a novel intersective way method (i-way), which uses intersection results of two machine learning algorithm namely, K-nearest neighbors (KNN) and Term frequency–inverse document frequency (TF-IDF). i-way is a 2-level extraction framework which represents win-win situation by considering intersective results of two different approaches to ensure that selection is progressing towards desired requirement for reuse consideration. The validity and effectiveness of results of proposed framework are evaluated on requirement dataset (Shaukat et al., 2018), which show that proposed approach can significantly help in reducing effort by selecting similar requirements of interest for reuse. Chapter 3 proposes a methodology for achieving requirement traceability and thereby performing requirement based testing for efficient test and evaluation of aircraft subsystems. This methodology integrates requirement traceability throughout the software development life cycle along with requirement based testing for high integrity software systems. The methodology has been found to be most effective in revealing errors and optimizes testing by preventing repetition of test cases across test platforms. This unique contribution has the potential to revolutionize the research world in software engineering. Chapter 4 undertakes a study to identify and analyze existing risk assessment and management techniques from a historical perspective that address and study risk management and perception of risk. The paper present extensive summary of existing literature on various techniques and approaches related to requirements defects, defect taxonomy, its classification and its potential impact on software development as the main contributions of this research work. The primary objective of this study was to present a systematic literature review of techniques/methods/tools for risk assessment and management. This research successfully identifies and discovers existing risk assessment and management techniques, their limitations, taxonomies, processes and identifies possible improvements for better defect identification and prevention. Chapter 5 is aimed at studying the key performance indicators of team members working in an Agile project environment and in an Extreme Programming software development. Practitioners from six different XP projects were selected to respond to the survey measuring the performance indicators, namely, escaped defects, team member's velocity, deliverables and extra efforts. The chapter presents a comparative view of Scrum and XP, the two renowned agile methods with their processes, methodologies, development cycles and artifacts while assessing the base performance indicators in XP setup. These indicators are key to any Agile project in a Global Software Development environment. The observed performance indicators were compared against the Gold Standard industry benchmarks along with best, average and worst case scenarios. Practitioners from six Agile XP projects were asked to participate in the survey. Observed results best serve the practitioners to take necessary course corrections to stay in the best case scenarios of their respective projects. Chapter 6 proposes an algorithm to make the bidding dynamic by not only awarding tenders on basis of cost quoted in tenders (biding cost) but also on contractor ratings. The ratings of contractor is computed using historical performance of contractor. The paper empirically identifies the factors to rate the contractors. The historical values associated with the performance rating parameters are then combined using the "controlled values" which one assumed to standard across the industry, to yield the overall weighted rating of firms. This rating is then combined with the bidding cost, thereby making the selection of contractor dynamic. Selected Contractor is paid bidding cost. The algorithm is executed a hypothetical value to illustrate the approach. A web application has been developed to execute the proposed algorithm. Chapter 7 surveys the quality improvement techniques for the two fundamental artifacts of software product development namely the architecture design and the source code. The information from top level research databases is compiled and an overall picture of quality enhancement in current software trends during the design, development and maintenance phases are presented. This helps both the software developers and the quality analysts to gain understanding of the current state of the art for quality improvement of design and source code and the usage of various practices. The results indicate the need for more realistic, precise, automated technique for architectural quality analysis. The complex nature of the current software products require the system developed to be beyond robust and resilient and building intelligent software that is anti-fragile, self-adaptive is favored. Innovative proposals that reduce the cost and time are invited. Chapter 8 presents a tool based on an analysis of different popular prototyping tools in the industry which will overcome some or all of the major issues faced by application designers. Author's describe the prototyping tool's concept, design, features as well as how it is suitable for making great user interfaces helping application designers to design exactly what they want. Chapter 9 proposed an algorithm to provide a proper way for the contractors to estimate the accurate cost of the project for which they provides bids. A survey was conducted to gather information about how the contractors generally estimate the cost of their project, problems they face in this process, their past experiences, factors they consider when estimating the cost of the project, etc. This chapter provides an effective solution to the problem of inaccurate cost estimation. The objective is to enhance the chances of the estimation of the final cost of the project that contractor believes it will incur, at the time of bidding. A web application has been developed to execute the proposed algorithm.

Chapter 10 describes the IV&V methodology for Field Programmable Gate Arrays (FPGA) based Design during the development Life Cycle along with the Certification Process.

This book contains research articles targeted various areas of software engineering like requirement management, quality, software testing, software approaches in civil engineering, agile teams, process models etc. The emergence of crowd sourcing had further enhanced the challenges that software engineer faced by enhancing the quantity of inputs for decision makings and forcing him to consider the human side of crowds (like motivation) to enhance quality of inputs. Crowd sourcing had beneficial role to play in software engineering as it provides software engineer the ability to consider the expectation of crowds and this may affect the software acceptability among them.

Varun Gupta
University of Beira Interior, Covilha, Portugal

Acknowledgment

ज्ञानशक्तिसिमारूढः तत्त्वमालावभूषितिः ।
भुक्तिमुक्तिप्रदाता च तस्मै श्रीगुरवे नमः ॥

First of all, I would like to thank my Gurus Prof. Durg Singh Chauhan, Dr. Kamlesh Dutta and Prof. Thomas Hanne, whose guidance through out research degrees and thereafter as an individual researcher, had made it possible to successfully lead & complete the editorial process of a book effectively.

सर्वार्थसंभवो देहो जनतिः पोषितो यतः ।
न तयोर्यातिं निर्वेशं पित्रोरमत्र्यः शतायुषा ॥

Secondly I would like to thank my parents for their continuous support and faith in me. Its is because of their sacrifices that helped me reach this stage of life.

Third, I would like to take the opportunity to thank the authors who had contributed their research findings in this book. I thank them for considering this book as the suitable platform for dissemination of their research work.

Further, I thank the editorial review board members for managing time from their busy schedules, for undertaking the double blind review process of the submitted research articles.

I also take this opportunity to thank the IGI publishers and their Book development Team for all the help & cooperation in making this book a reality.

Last but not the least, I would also like to thank indebted to all whosoever have contributed in this book.

Varun Gupta
University of Beira Interior, Covilha, Portugal

Chapter 1

Markov Decision Theory-Based Crowdsourcing Software Process Model

Kamalendu Pal
City, University of London, UK

ABSTRACT

The word crowdsourcing, a compound contraction of crowd and outsourcing, was introduced by Jeff Howe in order to define outsourcing to the crowd. It is a sourcing model in which individuals or organizations obtain goods and services. These services include ideas and development of software or hardware, or any other business-task from a large, relatively open and often rapidly-evolving group of internet users; it divides work between participants to achieve a cumulative result. It has been used for completing various human intelligence tasks in the past, and this is an emerging form of outsourcing software development as it has the potential to significantly reduce the implementation cost. This chapter analyses the process of software development at a crowdsourced platform. The work analyses and identifies the phase wise deliverables in a competitive software development problem. It also proposes the use of Markov decision theory to model the dynamics of the development processes of a software by using a simulated example.

INTRODUCTION

Crowdsourcing is the Information Technology (IT) mediated engagement of crowds for the purposes of problem-solving, task completion, idea generation and production (Howe, 2006; Howe, 2008; Brabham, 2008). The latest breakthroughs in Information and Communication Technologies (ICT) have ushered a new dawn for researchers to

DOI: 10.4018/978-1-5225-9659-2.ch001

design innovative crowdsourcing systems that can harness Human Intelligence Tasks (HITs) of online communities. The prime aim of crowdsourcing is to facilitate the *wisdom of crowds*. The theory suggests that the average response of many people, even amateurs, to a question is frequently more accurate than the view of a few experts. In this respect, a community of individuals with common interests and facing the same tasks can deliver better products and solutions than experts alone in the field. Information systems scholars Jean-Fabrice Lebraty and Katia Lobre-Lebraty confirmed that the *"diversity and impudence of the members of a crowd"* is a value addition to crowdsourcing operations (Lebraty & Lobre-Lebraty, 2013).

Therefore, the advantages of crowdsourcing lie mainly in the innovative ideas and problem-solving capacity that the diverse contributors – which may consist of experts and interested amateurs – can provide. The crowd can provide expert and faster solution to an existing problem. Depending on the challenge at hand, the solution provided may also prove innovative. In this way, crowdsourcing has emerged as a new labour pool for a variety of tasks, ranging from micro-tasks on Amazon Mechanical Turk (mTurk) to big innovation contests conducted by Netflix and Innocentive. Amazon mTurk today dominates the market for crowdsourcing small task that would be too repetitive and too tedious for an individual to accomplish. Amazon mTurk established a marketplace where requesters can post tasks and workers complete them for relatively small amount of money. Image tagging, document labeling, characterizing data, transcribing spoken languages, or creating data visualizations, are all tasks that are now routinely being completed online using the Amazon mTurk marketplace, providing higher speed of completion and lower price than in-house solutions.

Competitive crowdsourcing is reward based and has been used for variety of tasks from design of T-Shirts to research and development of pharmaceuticals and very recently for developing software (Howe, 2008; Lakhani & Lonstein, 2011; Stol & Fitzgerald, 2014).The mTurk is one of the best-known crowdsourcing platforms where HITs or microtasks are performed by thousands of workers (Ipeirotis, 2009).

There are different types of crowdsourcing platforms, such as virtual labour markets (VLMs), tournament crowdsourcing (TC) and open collaboration (OC), which each have different roles and characteristics (Estelles-Arolas & Gonzalez-Ladron-de-Guevara, 2012; Prpic, Taeihagh & Melton, 2014). Along with the growth of crowdsourcing, crowdsourcing platforms are very important to mediate the transactions. At the same time, IT-mediated platforms improve efficiency and decrease transaction costs and information asymmetry. However, these platforms are domain specific.

Crowdsourced Software Engineering derives from crowdsourcing. Using an open call, it recruits global online labour to work on different types of software engineering works, such as requirement elicitation, design, coding and testing.

This emerging model has been claimed to reduce time-to-market by increasing parallelism (Lakhani et al., 2010; LaToza et al., 2013; Stol & Fitzgerald, 2014), and to lower costs and defect rates with flexible development capability (Lakhani et al., 2010). Crowdsourced Software Engineering is implemented by many successful crowdsourcing platforms, such as TopCoder, AppStori, uTest, Mob4Hire and TestFlight. Crowdsourced Software Engineering has also rapidly gained increasing interest in both industrial and academic communities.

In this chapter only, software development related crowdsourcing business activities and relevant platforms are considered. Software development is creative and ever evolving. Organizations use various software development process models and methodologies for developing software. A software process model (SPM) specifies the stages in which a project should be divided, order of execution of these stages, and other constraints and conditions on the execution of these stage (Sommerville, 2017). However, the software development methodology (also known as SDM) framework did not emerge until the 1960s. The system development life cycle (SDLC) is the oldest formalized framework for building information systems. The main idea of the SDLC has been "to pursue the development of information systems in a very deliberate, structured and methodical way, requiring each stage of the life cycle – from inception of the idea to delivery of the final system – to be carried out rigidly and sequentially (Elliott, 2004) within the context of the framework being applied. The main objective of this framework in the 1960s was to develop large scale functional business systems in an age of large-scale business conglomerates, whose information systems activities revolved around heavy data processing and number crunching routines.

It is worth to explore strategies for successful use of software engineering and look at the history that forms the basic understanding of good software design and development practices. The history is important because the basics seem to have been ignored in many 1990s commercial enterprises seeking to develop large and complex software systems. In October 1968, a NATO conference on software engineering was held in Garmisch, Germany (Nauer & Randell, 1969). The conference organizers coined the phrase '*software engineering*' as a provocative term to "imply the need for software manufacture to be based on theoretical foundations and practical disciplines traditional to engineering". The highlights of the conference were discussions related to process: how to produce quality software efficiently, how to provide customer-oriented service, and how to protect a business investment in software. Good software engineering was equated with good project management.

As a matter of fact, software engineers aim to use software development models for building software that meets user requirements and is delivered within the specified time limit and budget. The objective of software crowdsourcing is to produce high quality and low-cost software products by harnessing the power of crowd. To meet this objective, the crowd workers who agree to work on the task are given some financial or social incentives (Hoffmann, 2009). The tasks could be executed in a collaborative or competitive manner based on the organization style. Wikipedia and Linux are viewed as well-known collaborative crowdsourcing examples (Howe, 2008; Doan, 2011). Developing a software through crowdsourcing blurs the distinction between a user and developer and follows a cocreation principle (Tsai, Wu, & Huhns, 2014).

With the increasing interest in crowdsourcing software development, it is significant to analyze the development process methodology used by crowdsourcing platforms. This chapter analyzes the process of software development at a crowdsourced platform. The work identifies various artifacts needed at each development phase and the order of events that occur along with the deliverables of each phase. The development process is modeled using a Markov Decision Process (MDP) that provides a mathematical framework for modelling decision making in situations where outcomes are partly random and partly under the control of the decision-maker. The reminder of this chapter is organized as follows. Section 2 introduces the background information of crowdsourcing. Section 3 presents a literature review. Section 4 describes the application development process of a crowdsourced platform. Section 5 explains the basis of modelling the process. Section 6 depicts the Markov Decision Process representation; and finally, Section 7 provides concluding remarks and future direction this research.

BACKGROUND OF CROWDSOURCING

The term 'crowdsourcing' was coined by Jeff Howe in 2006 through an article in the wired magazine as "the act of a company or institution taking a function once performed by employees and outsourcing it to an undefined (and generally large) network of people in the form of an open call" (Howe, 2006). The activities are executed by people who do not necessarily known each other, and interact with the company, the 'requester', via virtual tools and an internet connection. They become 'the workers': they can access tasks, execute them, upload the results and receive various forms of payment using any web browser. This is a labour market open 24/7, with a diverse workforce available to perform tasks quickly and cheaply.

A diagrammatic representation of well-established crowdsourcing platform Amazon's Mechanical Turk (mTurk) - (www.mturk.com) is shown in Figure 1. In this diagram, the "requesters" both design and post tasks for the Crowd to work on. In mTurk, tasks given to the "workers" are called Human Intelligence Tasks" (HITs). Requesters can test workers before allowing them to accept task and establish a baseline performance level of prospective workers. Requesters can also accept,

Figure 1. Schematic diagram of Amazon's Mechanical Turk system

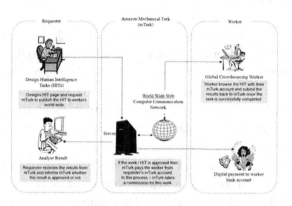

or reject, the results submitted by the workers, and this decision impacts on the worker's reputation within the mTurk system. Payments for completed tasks can be redeemed as 'Amazon.com' gift certificates or alternatively transferred to a worker's bank account. Details of the mTurk interface design, how an API is used to creates and post HITs and a description of the workers' characteristics are beyond the scope of this chapter. With each result submitted by a worker the requester receives an answer that including various information about how the task was processed. One element of this data is a unique "workerID" allowing the requester to distinguish between individual workers. Using this "workerID" it is possible to analyse how many different HITs each worker completed.

A definitive classification of Crowdsourcing tasks has not yet been established, however Corney and colleagues (Corney et al., 2010) suggest three possible categorizations based upon: nature of the task (creation, evaluation and organization tasks), nature of the crowd ('expert', 'most people' and 'vast majority') and nature of the payment (voluntary contribution, rewarded at a flat rate and rewarded with a prize). Similarly, Crowdsourcing practitioners, such as Chaordix (from the Cambrian House (www.cambrianhouse.com)) describes Crowdsourcing models as a Contest (i.e. individual submit ideas and the winner is selected by the company, 'the requester'), a Collaboration (i.e. individuals submit their ideas or results, the crowd evolves the ideas and picks a winner), and Moderated (i.e. individuals submit their ideas, the crowd evolves those ideas, a panel – set by 'the requesters' select the finalists and the crowd votes on a winner). In recent decades academics across many different disciplines have started reporting the use of Internet Crowdsourcing to support a range of research projects, e.g. social network motivators (Brabham, 2008), relevance of evaluations and queries (Alonso & Mizzaro, 2009; Kostakos, 2009), accuracy in judgment and evaluations (Kittur et al., 2008). Some of relevant research issues are described in the next section.

REVIEW OF LITERATURE

Since the coining of the term crowdsourcing, studies have been carried out on different aspects of crowdsourcing. Researchers have analyzed the economics of crowdsourcing contests, proposed models for pricing strategies and done analysis on earning reward and reputation, in general. Huberman (Huberman, 2009) analyzed data set from YouTube and demonstrate that the productivity exhibited in crowdsourcing exhibits a strong positive dependence on attention, measured by the number of downloads (Huberman, Romero, & Wu, 2008).

The purpose of this literature review section is two-fold: (i) Firstly, to provide a comprehensive survey of the current research progress on using crowdsourcing to support software engineering activities. (ii) Secondly, to summarize the challenges for Crowdsourced Software Engineering and to reveal to what extent these challenges were addressed by existing work. Since this field is an emerging, fast-expanding area in software engineering yet to achieve full maturity. The including literature may directly crowdsource software engineering tasks to the general public, indirectly reuse existing crowdsourced knowledge, or propose a framework to enable the realization or improvement of Crowdsourced Software Engineering.

In simplistic sense, the term 'Crowdsourced Software Engineering' to denote the application of crowdsourcing techniques to support software development. It emphasizes any software engineering activity included, thereby encompassing activities that do not necessarily yield software in themselves. For example, activities include project management, requirement elicitation, security augmentation and software test case generation and refinement. The studies specifying the use of crowdsourcing for developing software are few in literature. In his work Vukoic M (Vukoic, 2009) presented a sample crowdsourcing scenario in software development domain to derive the requirements for delivering a general-purpose crowdsourcing service in the Cloud (Vukovic, 2009). LaToza and colleagues (LaToza et al., 2014) developed an approach to decompose programming work into micro tasks for crowdsourced software development (Latoza, Towne, & Adriano, 2014). In their work Stol and Fitzgerald (2014) presented an industry case study of crowdsourcing software development at a multinational corporation and highlighted the challenges faced (Stol & Fitzgerald, 2014). Zhenghui H. and Wu W. (2014) applied the famous game theory to model the 2-player algorithm challenges on TopCoder (Hu & Wu, 2014).

Crowdsourced Software Engineering has several potential advantages compared to traditional software development methods. Crowdsourcing may help software development organizations integrate elastic, external human resources to reduce cost from internal employment, and exploit the distributed production model to speed up the development process.

For example, compared to conventional software development, the practice of TopCoder's crowdsourced software development was claimed to exhibit the ability to deliver customer requested software assets with a lower defect rate at lower cost in less time (Lakhni et al., 2010). TopCoder claimed that their crowdsourced development could reduce cost by 30% - 80% when compared with in-house development or outsourcing (Lydon, 2012). Furthermore, in the TopCoder American Online case study (Lakhani et al., 2010), the defect rate was reported to be 5 to 8 time lower compared with traditional software development practices.

In another study published in Nature Biotechnology (Lakhani et al., 2013), Harvard Medical School adopted Crowdsourced Software Engineering to improve DNA sequence gapped alignment search algorithms. With a development period of two weeks, the best crowd solution was able to achieve higher accuracy and three orders of magnitude performance improvement in speed, compared to the US National Institutes of Health's MegaBLAST.

The work on competitive crowdsourcing for developing software is in its infancy and our work analyses the development process model and build a Markov Decision Process (MDP) representation of the system. MDP has been widely used for representing sequential decision making and applied to wide range of problems for obtaining optimal solutions. Researchers in the past have used MDP to find optimal scheduling policy for a software project (Padberg, 2004); and for the assessment of the quality of the developed software (Korkmaz, Akman, & Ostrovska, 2014).

CROWDSOURCED PROCESS MODEL

Different crowdsourcing platforms are available for the development of software applications. Business enterprises like RentACoder, oDesk, Elance, Topcoder, uTest adopt different approaches for crowdsourcing (Hu & Wu, 2014). This chapter focuses on the development methodology used by TopCoder. This section presents that how software is developed through crowdsourcing, and the different phases of development along with the deliverables of each phase and the sequence of activities followed.

Software Application Development Methodology

TopCoder founded by Jack Hughes is one of the largest competition-based software development-portal that posts software developed tasks as contests (TopCoder, 2018) (Hu & Wu, 2014). With over 700,000 members it is one of the world's largest competitive crowdsourcing community (TopCoder, 2018). It has online community of digital creators who compete to develop and refine technology, web asserts, extreme value analytics, and mobile applications for customers (Begel, Bosh, & Storey, 2013).

Contests on the TopCoder platform are conducted under three categories: Algorithm Contests, Client Software Development Contests and Design Contests (Lakhani & Lonstein, 2011). The algorithm contests are conducted through single round matches that are posted fortnightly and attract many contestants. This study concerns the client software development contests that are conducted on this platform. Development of real-world complex systems is broken into a variety of competitions and the development proceeds through distinct phases of these competitions. TopCoder provides mechanisms and infrastructure to manage and facilitate the creation of problem statements and their solutions. A platform manager is assigned to each project who closely works with the client to formulate the problem and host it onto the platform in the form of competitions. The software application development methodology at the TopCoder platform is shown in the Figure 2.

Phase Specific Deliverables

The application development process progresses in phases. Each phase is executed through a competition or a series of competitions and the winning entry serves as an input to the subsequent phases. The client of a crowdsourced platform may use an existing component from the platform catalogue or request for creation of a new component. There are six broad phases namely – Conceptualization, Specification, Architecture, Component Design and Development, Testing and Assembly.

Conceptualization

The competitions under Conceptualization phase are conducted to identify and document the needs and ideas of the project stakeholders. These competitions can commence by either running a series of Studio competitions to create graphical conceptualization artifacts like Storyboards, Wireframes and Prototypes, or a series of Conceptualization contests to create a Business Requirement Document and High-Level Use Cases.

After the component design competition is completed, the detailed component design specifications act an input into Component development competition. During this competition the component is implemented.

Specification

During the Specification competitions, the application requirements are formulated in as much detail as necessary in order to accomplish the goals for this application module. The high-level use cases that are identified during Conceptualization contests are assigned to modules during System Architecture phase, and during the

Figure 2. Software application development methodology

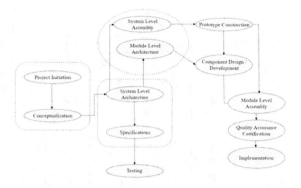

Specification phase all the individual scenarios that make up those use cases are broken up in text and graphical form using UML Activity Diagrams.

Architecture

The System Level Architecture competition takes the business requirements and prototype defined in conceptualization phase as input to define the overall technical approach that will be employed to meet those requirements. Module-Level Architecture Phase defines the lower-level technical design of an independent module of a larger application. This phase is responsible for defining the components and their interactions that will implement the requirements for the module.

Design and Development

During the component design competition, competitors get an opportunity to clarify any unclear requirements and define technical details for implementation. Component design competitions take the component requirements developed during the architecture phase as input and produce a detailed component design specification.

C: Client; UCD: Use Case Diagram; BRD: Business Requirement Document; CC: Conceptualization Competition; SC: Specification Competition; SDS: System Design Specification; ARS: Application Requirement Specification; SL_AC: System Level Architecture Competition; G-CC: Graphical Conceptualization Competition; ML-AC: Module Level Architecture Competition; TC: Testing Competition; ML-AYC: Module Level Assembly Competition

After the component design competition is completed, the detailed component design specifications act an input into Component development competition. During this competition the component is implemented.

Table 1. Phase Wise Deliverables

Software Development Phase	Input	Source	Related Artifacts as input	Related artifacts towards output	Deliverables
Conceptualization (CC)	Conceptualization Questionnaire	C	Wireframes / Storyboards	UCD	BRD Prototype
System Level Architecture (SL-AC)	BRD Activity Diagrams Technical Questionnaire	CC SC C	Storyboards / Wireframes / Prototype Technical Questionnaire	Sequence Diagram Interface Diagram	SDS Integration Plan
Specification (SC)	Conceptualization Documents High level Use Cases Specification Template	CC	Wireframes / Storyboards / Prototypes	Activity Diagram	ARS
Testing (TC)	BRD SDS	CC SL-AC	Activity Diagrams / Use Cases / Prototypes	Test Scripts	QA Plan Application test suite
Module Level Architecture (ML-AC)	BRD Storyboards / Wireframes / Protype Activity Diagram Technical Questionnaire	CC G-CC SC C	Wireframes / Storyboards / Prototypes	Module Sequence Diagrams / Module Interface Diagrams	Module Design Specifications / Component Requirement Specifications
System Level Assembly (SL-AYC)	BRD System Level Architecture	SC SL-AC	Prototype	Deployment Document	Assembly Source
Protype Assembly (P-AYC)	Application Specification Documents	C	Prototype	Deployment Document	Assembly Code
Component Design / Development (CDDC)	Component Specification	SL-AC ML-AC	Component Design Requirements	Unit Tests	Component Design CGC Component Documentation

continues on following page

Table 1. Continued

Software Development Phase	Input	Source	Related Artifacts as input	Related artifacts towards output	Deliverables
Module Level Assembly (ML-AYC)	BRD UCD Activity Diagram QA Plan Application Design Specification Component Sequence and Deployment Diagram	CC SC TC ML-AC	Custom and Generic Components	Deployment Document	Assembly Source
Certification	Completed Assembly Requirement Documents	ML-AYS SC	Test Cases	JIRA Issues	Bug Fixes

Testing

Testing competitions provide the mechanism for verifying that the requirements identified during the initial phases of the project were properly implemented and that the system performs as expected. The test scenarios developed through these competitions ensures that the requirements are met end-to-end.

Assembly

The System Assembly competition creates the foundation for the application. This includes creating the build scripts that will be used throughout the application as well as incorporating all identified components into the shell that implements the application's cross-cutting corners. The Prototype Assembly competition focuses on the logic and functionality required as part of the front end and converts a prototype into the presentation-layer shell of the application. This competition is run after the protype has been approved by the client. Since this competition does not focus on back-end functionality or architecture, it can be run before or during the architecture phase.

Module Assembly competition integrates components developed during the component production process into the shell application built during System Assembly. The core functionality of the application is put in place and a fully-functional application is an output of this phase. After the application is assembled, certification verifies that the application functions correctly. Using the test cases produced by Testing Competitions, as well as Bug Hunt Competitions, the application is compared to the requirements for the purpose of Validation. Table 1 shows the major deliverables from the various phases of the development process.

Activity Sequence

The platform also provides a service called 'TopCoderDirect', which is more like a self-service mode in which there is no intervention of the employees of TopCoder. In this service, a platform manager acts as a Co-pilot to educate the client on the working of the platform and the hosting of the competitions is done directly by the client. A Co-pilot or a Platform Manager who is assigned to a project has the responsibility of hosting the competitions of each phase and each phase of the development process follows the sequence of activities as listed in Figure 3.

The setup activity is undertaken before the competition is posted and on an average is of 02 days duration. Once the competition is posted, the registration time duration of around two days is given to the competitors to register for the competition. The competitors after registering for the event work on developing their solution for

Figure 3. Activity sequence

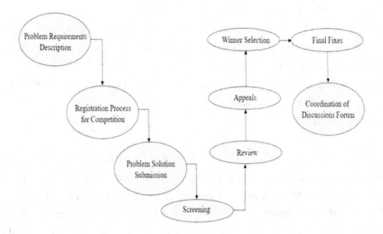

around one to five days. The competitors may ask queries or discuss their problems in the forum, before submitting the solution. After the submission phase closes, quick screening of the submitted solutions is done as per the minimum quality standards set by the platform to decide eligible entries to the review phase. A panel of three members then reviews each solution that has passed the screening on a scorecard. The process takes around a day and after its completion, the competitors get an opportunity to appeal for anything they believe to be an error in scoring. The time duration for making an appeal is around a day. After the appeal process is completed, the final score of each submission is calculated and a winner is declared based on the highest score submission. The winner then may address any issues that were identified during the review process and after the final fixes and review the winning contestant is required to support a contest by answering forum questions for that contest.

Advantages

The competition-based development model used by TopCoder has successfully created software for the use of individuals and organizations. Some of the benefits of the competition-based development model to a project in an organization are as listed below:

- The time and cost needed to hire, train and fire people are lowered.
- The cost of networking, communication and infrastructure is reduced.
- The participants possess diverse skills and experience there by creating innovative solutions.

- The individual's interest and choice of working on a problem increases the chances of submitting solutions as per the deadline.
- The solutions to the problems are not depend on individuals.
- The intensive review process ensures the selection of the best and quality work as a winning solution.
- Winning solution is rewarded with a fixed pre-decided amount only if the solution meets the specifications and is delivered on time there by reducing cost of development.

There are numerous benefits that crowd workers realize to be active participants in the competition-based development model. Individuals are keen to participate a competitor either to spend quality time on the internet for fun or to earn extra income. The social and financial incentives gained by competitors are often a driving factor for continuous participation in the competitions at a crowdsourced platform. The flexibility of working as per their convenience and having no requirement of reporting to their bosses is an attraction for many.

System Modelling

It is important to model the behavior of the system to demonstrate progression and evaluate performance. Markov Decision Process (MDP) is a useful technique to abstract the model of dynamics of the development process (16). This section formalizes the software development process as an MDP which represents a way of modelling a system, through states and transition. An MDP is a discrete time stochastic control process, formally presented by a tuple of four objects (S, A, Pa_i, Ra_i) (19). S is the state space; $s \in S$ is the current state of the system. A is the action space, where $a_i \in A$ is the action taken based on the current state. P_{a_i} (s, s') is the probability that action a_i in state s at time t will lead to state s' at time t + 1. Ra_i is the immediate reward obtained on performance action a_i.

Software development process occurs in phases and a phase ends when the deliverables of that phase have been produced and this characteristic of the phase allows us to use a discrete-time, MDP as a mathematical model. This chapter presents the software development process that has been adopted as a sequential decision problem in which the set of actions, rewards, cost, and transition probabilities depend only on the current state of the system and the current action being performed. In a crowdsourced software development methodology, a platform manager works with the client to formulate a project road map for building the software. The development then progresses in phases from conceptualization contests in order to finalize BRD, to conducting a series of specification contests to finalize ARS and developing application's wireframes and storyboards, to conducting architecture contests for final SDS and for creation of new components through design and development competitions towards assembly competitions, generation of QA plan through testing competitions and eventually deployment. In this chapter the development process is built in a way that different states and an action results in the transition from one state to another.

States

The state of a system is a parameter, that describes the system. The state of software project changes at the end of each phase. The state consists of four parts:

1. A status vector (V)
2. An accomplishment vector (V_a)
3. A progress vector (P)
4. A countdown variable (C)

The status vector has an entity for each component that defines the status of the component. As the development progresses the project moves from initialization towards completion. There are many artifacts, intermediate deliverables and components that are developed as the project progresses. The status of these components can have any of the following values:

* ND; Not Developed
* TD: To be Developed
* UQ: Under Qualification
* AD: Almost Developed
* SD: Successfully Developed
* CD: Cancelled Development

The set of all possible status values would be {ND, TD, UD, UQ, AD, SD, CD}. The ND state is the initial state of the component. The TD state is a state when the development has not yet started but is in pipeline/ The UD state is the state in which the component is being developed. The UQ is the under-qualification state of the component where qualification is termed as the criteria for deciding the component to qualify for the acceptance. The AD state is a state when the development is almost completed but needs final fixes before completion. The SD state is termed as the completion of the component. CD state represent a cancelled development status of the component.

The status vector of a project defines the status of project components:

$$V = (v_1, v_2, v_3, \ldots, v_z, \ldots v_N)$$

where v_z represents the status of the zth project component at the end of the current phase and N is the total number of project components. For example, the vector (TD, UQ, SD) can be considered a valid status vector for a project having three components.

The accomplishment vector V_a is the contestant ID who is a wining contestant and has successfully accomplished the task of developing a component. It has a value of 0 if no contestant is a winning contestant for successful development of the component so far. For example, the vector (1, 3, 0) can be considered a valid assignment vector for a project having three components. The progress vector P defines the time that has been spent working on a component in a phase. If the work is completed on the component and it has been successfully developed the value of P would be infinity. If the competition has been set up and no submissions have been received, then the value would be 0.

Every project has a deadline and the platform manager in consultation with the client establishes an estimated development time for a project. The countdown variable c is the time left for the completion of the project as per the predetermined development time.

Actions

An action defines what is done with the project deliverable at a given development phase. Actions may depend on the current state and phase of development. On performing a particular action, the state is changed to a new state. The new state of the component depends on what action is performed. The possible actions that can be performed based on the activity sequence as discussed in previous section are as stated below:

1. Reuse existing component (a_1)
2. Setting-up Competition
   a. Reviewing Requirements to setup (a_2)
   b. Establishing Project Goals (a_3)
   c. Identifying Important Processes (a_4)
   d. Contest Posting (a_5)
   e. Cancelling Contest (a_6)
3. Registration and Submission
   a. Member registration for Competition (a_7)

      b.   Forum Discussion (a_8)

      c.   Submission of solution by registered competitors (a_9)

      d.   Submission Closed (a_{10})

      e.   Screening of the submission (a_{11})

      f.   Cancelling Contest (a_6)

4.   Reviewing

      a.   Reviewing of screened submissions (a_{12})

      b.   Evaluating scorecard (a_{13})

      c.   Addressing appeals (a_{14})

      d.   Selecting Winner (a_{15})

      e.   Final Fixes and Reviews (a_{16})

      f.   Winning Contestant Support (a_{17})

      g.   4. g. Cancelling Contest (a_6)

$A = \{a_1, a_2, a_3, \dots a_{17}\}$

Transition Probabilities

The transition probability, P_{ai} (s, s') represents the probability of a system to move from one state, s to another s' under a stated action a_i. The next state is not determined alone by the stochastic nature of selected dynamics, it occurs with some probability. We have assumed the transition probability from a Not Developed (ND) state to Successfully Developed (SD) state directly, on choosing to reuse a component from the existing catalogue of the platform and not entering the development phases. We have assumed the probabilities based on the statistical data as published in the literature. According to the case study (7), 60 percent of the times a reusable component is selected from the existing catalogue. It is assumed that the remaining 40 percent of the times the development progress through competitions, 90 percent of the times the progression is smooth and 10 percent of the times, the progression encounter issues to cancel and roll back competitions.

Immediate Reward

Moving from one state to another on taking a particular action a_i, results in getting an immediate reward Ra_i. The reward can be positive or negative number from a set of real numbers R. In the present model, it has been assumed that moving from one state to another represents progression and an immediate stationary reward of positive 5 units is attained uniformly for all states when progression is towards completion. Any cancelling action undertaken during the development of a component at any state, results in a negative reward of 5 units, as it depicts cost incurred and penalty. Since development is a time-based process, it is to be noted that the impact of cancelling contest during a latest stage of development results in more loss as compared to the early states.

MDP REPRESENTATION AND RESULTS

An MDP model is given in Figure 3. The circle represents the state of the component at a given time t in the system. The edges represent the chosen action that causes the state to be changed and depicts admissible transition. The probability of a system to move to new resultant state (s') at time (t + 1) after a stated action is taken is depicted along with the edges. The representation of various states is as follows: State 0: ND; State 1: TD; State 2: UD; State 3: CD; State 4: UQ; State 5: AD; State 6: SD. The Transition probability Maximum and the Immediate Reward Matrix are given at Table 2 and Table 3 respectively.

Table 2. Transition probability matrix

To From	State 0	State 1	State 2	State 3	State 4	State 5	State 6
State 0	0.0	0.4	0.0	0.0	0.0	0.0	0.6
State 1	0.0	0.0	0.9	0.1	0.0	0.0	0.0
State 2	0.0	0.0	0.0	0.1	0.9	0.0	0.0
State 3	0.0	0.0	0.0	0.0	0.0	0.0	0.0
State 4	0.0	0.0	0.0	0.1	0.0	0.9	0.0
State 5	0.0	0.0	0.0	0.0	0.0	0.0	1.0
State 6	0.0	0.0	0.0	0.0	0.0	0.0	0.0

Table 3. Transition probability matrix

To From	State 0	State 1	State 2	State 3	State 4	State 5	State 6
State 0		5					
State 1			5	-5			
State 2				-10	5		
State 3							
State 4				-15		5	
State 5							5
State 6							

Figure 4. MDP representation of the model

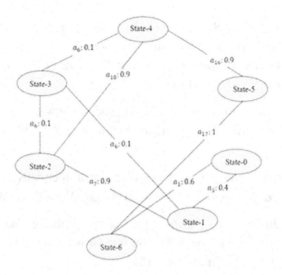

CONCLUSION AND FUTURE WORK

IT enterprises these days are keen on crowdsourcing the tasks to their internal employees for optimal utilization of their resources. In times to come we may see a total change in the way software is being developed. Rather than hiring people for specific tasks and creating a workforce, or crowdsourcing to their own employees, organizations might switch to this peer production mode of getting software developed through genera crowd. There being limited studies on the development process models for developing software, the presented work provides an insight into the various phase, deliverables and integration strategies resulting into a final product. This chapter modeled the development process as a Markov Decision Process and present different states a component can be in, probably actions and their resulting states.

In the long term, the methods presented here could also be used for building up databases of 'solutions and decisions' that machine intelligence requires. In other words, an Internet crowd could be used for the generation "cases", by exposing them to decision-making situations the system will encounter. Once analyzed and amalgamated, these could be stored and embedded into the system's knowledge bases, from which they can be pulled and put into action when necessary. In this way the crowd, a "knowledge network", becomes the solution provider. The proposed model would enable to depict and monitor the progress of development of software through a crowdsourced platform. The extension of the work would be a stochastic simulation of the proposed model is to estimate the optimal scheduling strategies for developing software through a crowdsourced platform.

REFERENCES

Alonso, O., & Mizzaro, S. (2009). Relevance criteria for e-commerce: a Crowdsourcing-based experimental analysis. *Proceedings of the 32nd International ACM SIGIR Conference on Research and Development in Information Retrieval*, 760-761. 10.1145/1571941.1572115

Begel, A., Bosh, J., & Storey, M. A. (2013). Social Networking Meets Software Development: Perspectives from GitHub. *Software, 30*(1), 52–66. doi:10.1109/MS.2013.13

Brabham, D. C. (2008). Crowdsourcing as a model for problem solving an introduction and cases. *Convergence, 14*(1), 75–90. doi:10.1177/1354856507084420

Brabham, D. C. (2008a). Moving the crowd at iStockphoto: The composition of the crowd and motivations for participation in a Crowdsourcing application. *First Monday, 13*(6). doi:10.5210/fm.v13i6.2159

Corney, J. R., Torres-Sanchez, C., Jagadeesan, A., Prasanna, R., & William, C. (2010). Outsourcing labour to the cloud. *International Journal of Innovation and Sustainable Development, 4*(4), 294–313. doi:10.1504/IJISD.2009.033083

Doan, A., Ramakrishnan, R., & Halevy, A. Y. (2011). Crowdsourcing systems on the World-Wide Web. *Communications of the ACM, 54*(4), 86. doi:10.1145/1924421.1924442

Elliott, G. (2004). *Global Business Information Technology: an integrated system approach*. Person Education Limited.

Estelles-Arolas, E., & Gonzalez-Lodron-De-Guevara, F. (2012). Towards an integrated crowdsourcing definition. *Journal of Information Science, 38*(2), 189–200. doi:10.1177/0165551512437638

Hoffmann, L. (2009). Crowd Control. *Communications of the ACM, 52*(3), 16–17. doi:10.1145/1467247.1467254

Howe, J. (2006). *The rise of crowdsourcing. Wired Magazine*.

Hu, Z., & Wu, W. (2014). A Game Theoretic Model of Software Crowdsourcing. In *Proceedings of Service Oriented System Engineering* (pp. 446–453). SOSE. doi:10.1109/SOSE.2014.79

Huberman, B. A., Romero, D. M., & Wu, F. (2009). Crowdsourcing – Attention and Productivity. *Information Science, 35*(6), 758–765. doi:10.1177/0165551509346786

Ipeirotis, P. G. (2009). *Analyzing the Amazon Mechanical Turk Marketplace*. ACM XRDS.

Kitur, A., Chi, E. H., & Suh, B. (2008). Crowdsourcing user studies with mechanical turk. In *Proceeding of the Twenty-sixth Annual SIGCHI Conference on Human Factors in Computer Systems*. ACM. 10.1145/1357054.1357127

Korkmaz, O., Akman, I., & Ostrovska, S. (2014). Assessing Software Quality Using the Markov Decision Processes. *Human Factors and Ergonomics in Manufacturing & Service Industries, 24*(1), 86–104. doi:10.1002/hfm.20355

Kostakos, V. (2009). Is the crowd's wisdom biased? A quantitative analysis of three online communities. *International Symposium on Social Intelligence and Networking (SIN09)*, Vancouver, Canada. 10.1109/CSE.2009.491

Lakhani, K. R., Boudreau, K. J., Loh, P. R., Backstrom, L., Baldwin, C., Lonstein, E., ... Guinan, E. C. (2013). Prize-based contests can provide solutions to computational biology problems. *Nature Biotechnology, 31*(2), 108–111. doi:10.1038/nbt.2495 PMID:23392504

Lakhani, K. R., Garvin, D. A., & Lonstein, E. (2010). *TopCoder(A): Developing software through crowdsourcing*. Harvard Business School Case.

Lakhani, K. R. & Lonstein, E. (2011). *TopCoder(A): Developing Software through Crowdsourcing (TN)*. Harvard Business Teaching note, 611-671, March 2011.

Latoza, T. D., Ben Towne, W., Adriano, C. M., & Van Der Hock, A. (2014). Microtask Programming: Building Software with a Crowd. *User Interface Software and Technology Symposium*, 43-54. 10.1145/2642918.2647349

Lebraty, J., & Lobre-Lebraty, K. (2013). *Crowdsourcing: one Step Beyond*. London: John Wiley & Sons. doi:10.1002/9781118760765

Lydon, M. (2012). *Topcoder overview*. Retrieved from http://www.nasa.gov/pdf/651447main.TopCder_Mike_D1_830am.pdf

Nauer, P., & Randell, B. (1969). *Conference on Software Engineering*. NATO Scientific Affairs Division.

Padberg, F. (2004). Linking software process modelling with Markov decision theory. *Proceedings of the 28th Annual International Computer Software and Application Conference, COMPSAC 2004, 2*, 152-155.

Prpic, J., Taeihagh, A., & Melton, J. (2014). Experiments on Crowdsourcing, Policy Assessment. In *Proceeding of IPP 2014*. Oxford Internet Institute.

Puterman, M. L. (1994). Markov Decision Processes: Discrete Stochastic Dynamic Programming. Academic Press.

Sommerville, I. (2017). *Software Engineering*. Person Education Limited.

Stol, K., & Fitzgerald, B. (2014). Two's Company, Three's a Crowd: A Case Study of Crowdsourcing Software Development. *Proceedings of ICSE, 2014*, 187–198.

Stol, K., & Fitzgerald, B. (2014). Researching Crowdsourcing Software Development: Perspectives and Concerns. *Proceedings of CSI-SE*, 7-10. 10.1145/2593728.2593731

TopCoder. (2018). Available: http://www.topcder.com

Tsai, W. T., Wu, W., & Huhns, M. N. (2014). Cloud-Based Software Crowdsourcing. *Internet Computing, 18*(3), 78–83. doi:10.1109/MIC.2014.46

Vukovic, M. (2009). Crowdsourcing for Enterprises Maja Vukovi. Proceedings of Congess on Services-I, 686-692.

KEY TERMS AND DEFINITIONS-

Crowdsourcing: Crowdsourcing is the Information Technology mediated engagement of crowds for the purposes of problem-solving, task completion, idea generation, and production.

Crowdsourcing Software Engineering: Crowdsourcing software engineering derives from crowdsourcing. Using an open call, it recruits global online labour to work on different types of software engineering works, such as requirement elicitation, design, coding and testing.

Human Intelligence Tasks: In crowdsourcing business model, employers post jobs known as Human Intelligence Tasks (HITs), such as identifying specific content in an image or video.

Markov Decision Theory: In practice, decision is often made without a precise knowledge of their impact on future behaviour of systems under consideration. The field of Markov Decision Theory has developed a versatile approach to study and optimize the behaviour of random processes by taking appropriate actions that influence future evolution.

Software Process Model: In software engineering, a software process model is the mechanism of dividing software development work into distinct phases to improve design, product management, and project management. It is also known as a software development life cycle. The methodology may include the pre-definition of specific *deliverables* and *artifacts* that are created and completed by a project team to develop or maintain an application.

Chapter 2
I-Way:
A Cloud-Based Recommendation System for Software Requirement Reusability

Chetna Gupta
Jaypee Institute of Information Technology, Noida, India

Surbhi Singhal
Jaypee Institute of Information Technology, Noida, India

Astha Kumari
Jaypee Institute of Information Technology, Noida, India

ABSTRACT

This study addresses the problem of effectively searching and selecting relevant requirements for reuse meeting stakeholders' objectives through knowledge discovery and data mining techniques maintained over a cloud platform. Knowledge extraction of similar requirement(s) is performed on data and meta-data stored in central repository using a novel intersective way method (i-way), which uses intersection results of two machine learning algorithm namely, K-nearest neighbors (KNN) and term frequency-inverse document frequency (TF-IDF). I-way is a two-level extraction framework which represents win-win situation by considering intersective results of two different approaches to ensure that selection is progressing towards desired requirement for reuse consideration. The validity and effectiveness of results of proposed framework are evaluated on requirement dataset, which show that proposed approach can significantly help in reducing effort by selecting similar requirements of interest for reuse.

DOI: 10.4018/978-1-5225-9659-2.ch002

INTRODUCTION

Requirements reuse is a deliberate methodology which provides organizations with the novel ability to share a requirement crosswise over projects without absorbing unnecessary duplication of artifacts, thereby reducing development cost and accelerating time to market delivery. In last few years researchers and IT practitioners have attracted towards the concept of requirement reusability with the objective to decide on a set/subset of ready to use requirements ("as-is" or with some modifications). Though requirement reusability supports resource optimization during development and helps in reduction of errors but it is a challenging task that requires careful decision making and planning to provide desired functionality to the user. An early start preferably during requirement elicitation in this direction is most beneficial form of software reuse to save cost, time and accelerate time to market delivery. Decision on which requirement to reuse and to what extend depends upon the project context and situation at hand. Existence of a particular requirement does not guarantee that it is reusable in its present form. In the light of reusability, requirements are tuned to specific needs in order to increase their value to the customer and adaptability for the project at hand. Software developers should not only focus on the context in which an existing requirement can be used rather they should analyze other aspects of a requirement like, dependency between two or more requirements, related requirements that go well with the chosen one and might be reused along in order to add more value to the system, use cases, tests, attributes and hierarchy. In other words, a well written (at the right level of abstraction and scope) requirement should only be considered for reuse as comparison to generic requirements which might not save cost and time of software developers due to non availability of complete description of a requirement. Though it has received little attention (Kotonya & Sommerville, 1997; Lamsweerde, 2000), reusing early software products and processes can impact the life cycle from two basic points of view: improving the requirements engineering process (Cybulski, 1998; Sutcliffe et al., 1998), and supporting the development with reuse (Bellinzona et al., 1993; Bellinzona et al., 1992) process. Several tools and approaches for example, (Chou et al., 1996; Mannion et al., 1999; Mobasher & Cleland-Huang, 2009; Pacheco et al., 2017; Bakar et al., 2015; Schmitt & Liggesmeyer, 2015; Paydar & Kahani, 2015) etc. have been proposed in the literature to support requirement reuse as part of their functionality which can assist in finding a better set of software requirements according to a set of goals and constraints. Majority of them uses structuring and matching of requirements as a method. Other approaches use requirement specifications with similar behaviour or reuse, based on the assumption that specifications that exhibit similar behaviour are appropriate for reuse for the system which is under development.

Motivated by above observation, this paper proposes a multi-criteria requirement reusability tool which first elicits stakeholder preference value to understand the interest of project stakeholder. This further assists developers to select relevant requirements from shared requirement repository and design solution to meet stakeholder value with minimum cost and budget. This shared resource in fact is a repository from where similar requirements matching criteria are retrieved, modified to tune it according to the need of the current project that is subsequently stored back into repository. A cloud support with web application is provided to assists developers in selecting a requirement in an optimized way using K-nearest neighbors (KNN) and term frequency–inverse document frequency (TF-IDF) from requirement repository to assist large scale software project development. Requirement repository here refers to the collection of requirements which supports requirement selection procedure by considering three main parts of a requirement namely, data, metadata and their inter relationships. The whole process is divided into two levels: goal base (representing data part of requirement) and deep analysis base (representing metadata and relationship part of requirement) which stores details pertaining to their probable effort, risk and correlation among requirements. This 2-level extraction framework represents win-win situation by considering intersective results of two different machine learning approaches to ensure that selection is progressing towards desired requirement for reuse consideration.

The entire paper is organized as follows: A discussion on related work is presented in section 2. Detailed explanation of the proposed approach, tool support, result observation and research questions is discussed in section 3 and 4 respectively. The concluding remark follows in section 5.

Literature Review

The identification and timely reuse of requirements could potentially reduce development costs, shorten time-to-market, improve quality, and increase product competitiveness. (Chou et al., 1996) proposed an objective of behavior-based classification and retrieval technique for object-oriented specification reuse. Reusable requirements are identified using semantic similarity. The basis of their study was that specifications with similar behavior can be considered for reuse. In this study, data was collected using document examination and degree of reuse was the variable to be measured. (Woo & Robinson, 2002) have proposed an approach which relies on semantics of UML diagrams. Dataset was constructed using CASE tools. The variable measured was degree of reuse which gave a positive result. The whole approach was illustrated with the tool called SCENASST (SCENarioASSisTant), which uses machine learning techniques. Similar work is proposed by (Paydar & Kahani, 2015) uses UML diagrams to support reusability by measuring the similarity of UML-based use-cases through metric. (Benitti & da Silva, 2013) uses catalog of patterns and the traceability between requirements to support requirement reusability. Questionnaires were collected to construct dataset. Requirement management and degree of reuse were the measured variables which gave satisfactory result. Results were observed using both qualitative and quantitative analysis. (Moon et al., 2005) proposed an approach in which requirements are observed as core assets and they suggested a process model having four stages to develop and generate reusable requirements. Dataset was made by examining the documents. SPL suitability and degree of reuse variables were measured which gave positive result. (Eriksson et al., 2009) proposes a model called PLUSS which uses feature models to support requirement reuse. In their study, document examination is used to create dataset. Acceptability, degree of reuse, and SPL suitability variables were measured. It consisted of multiple data collections in order to address the research questions. (Maiden & Sutcliffe, 1992) proposed an approach which uses three step method to develop and reuse requirements for reuse. They collected data by examining the documents. Degree of reuse and development effort variables were measured. They discussed a case tool, Ira, to implement and describe the proposed approach. (Mannion et al., 1999) proposed an approach to reuse requirements based on application of families which uses requirements set, a domain model and discriminates to identify requirements for reuse. Data was collected by examining various documents. SPL suitability was the only variable to be measured. This study extends MARM model and uses TRAM tool to analyze results. (Pacheco et al., 2017) proposed an approach called Requirements reuse model for Software Requirements Catalog (RRMSRC) which is capable of supporting requirements reuse activities based on the IEE Std. 830- 1998 for maximizing the effectiveness of reuse by matching requirements to identify reusable requirements. This approach uses requirements catalog to support the requirements reuse (Pacheco et al., 2015). (Goldin & Berry, 2015) recommend a reuse procedure dependent on 'project families' that structure the requirements utilizing one of a kind naming. The examination portrays the experience from several contextual analyses of projects that have used reuse of requirements. A model presented by Schmitt and Liggesmeyer (Schmit & Liggesmeyer, 2015) structures the requirements for reuse under security requirements area only. These structures can enable reuse in different contexts. (Bakar et al., 2015) extracts high-frequency words from requirements through text mining to support the reuse of requirements. The examination portrays the strategy to build up the artefacts for reuse but the proposed approach yet does not exhibit how these newly extracted features will be reused. Many researchers have used Ivarsson and Gorschek's rubric (Ivarsson & Gorschek, 2011) and have provided various refinements to it for supporting reuse (Munir et al., 2014; Ali et al., 2014; Munir et al., 2016; Elberzhager et al., 2012).

S. Lim and A. Finkelstein (Lim et al., 2012) proposed StakeRare approach that uses social network analysis and collaborative filtering to identify and prioritize requirements in large software projects. Stakeholders are asked to rank initial requirements and new set of requirements are recommended using collaborative filtering approach. On similar lines two more approaches mentioned in (Castro-Herrera e al., 2008) and (Mobasher & Cleland-Huang, 2009) recommend requirements to stakeholders using collaborative filtering. The basis of recommendation is related to identifying stakeholders, generating requirements and providing support for decision making tasks. (Maalej & Thuremella, 2009) proposed a research agenda for recommendation systems in requirements engineering. They visualized potential uses of recommendation systems which included recommendation of quality measures, templates to use, past rationale decisions, vocabulary to use, requirements from previous systems, experts in domain for solving particular issues, status of activities and priority.

PROPOSED APPROACH

This study aims to identify and recommend requirements that are most similar to the initial, top ranked set of stakeholder's requirements. The proposed approach mines requirement description of data, meta data and their relationships from shared repository and uses text mining, k-Nearest- Neighbour and cosine similarity with Tf-Idf algorithms to recommend a new context specific requirement. The recommended requirements are analyzed for consideration of reusability which can relatively save cost and time of software developers.

Elicitation of Stakeholder's Priority

The process starts with assisting stakeholders in elicitation of their initial interest using a tool support to interleaves human activities using a multi criteria decision analysis method, TOPSIS (Hwang & Yoon, 1981) to obtain ideal preferences ranking on following five prime criteria's: business value importance, urgency, market influence, ease of use and volatility. Figure1 provides a snapshot of initial ordering generated for an example set of 10 requirements as stakeholders initial ordering for a web based project providing farming assistance to farmers. This model enhances business communication and facilitates direct communication between farmer-to-supplier and farmer-to-farmer. A total of 10 requirements selected as an independent module to carry out this work. These initial preferences will help software developers in deciding which among the set of requirements will be selected first as input for identifying similar requirements for reusability.

Figure 1. Snapshot of elicited of stakeholder's initial priority rankings

Requirements	Business Value					Urgency					market influence					ease of use					volatility					Requirements	Initial Ranking
	1	2	3	4	5	1	2	3	4	5	1	2	3	4	5	1	2	3	4	5	1	2	3	4	5		
R1	☐	☑	☐	☐	☐	☐	☐	☐	☑	☐	☐	☐	☐	☐	☑	☐	☐	☐	☑	☐	☐	☐	☐	☐	☑	R1	4
R2	☐	☐	☑	☐	☐	☐	☐	☐	☐	☑	☐	☑	☐	☐	☐	☑	☐	☐	☐	☐	☐	☑	☐	☐	☐	R2	7
R3	☐	☑	☐	☐	☐	☐	☐	☐	☐	☑	☐	☑	☐	☐	☐	☐	☐	☐	☑	☐	☑	☐	☐	☐	☐	R3	5
R4	☑	☐	☐	☐	☐	☐	☐	☑	☐	☐	☐	☐	☑	☐	☐	☐	☐	☐	☑	☐	☐	☐	☐	☐	☑	R4	2
R5	☐	☑	☐	☐	☐	☐	☐	☑	☐	☐	☐	☐	☐	☑	☐	☐	☐	☐	☑	☐	☐	☐	☐	☐	☑	R5	6
R6	☐	☐	☐	☑	☐	☐	☐	☐	☑	☐	☐	☐	☐	☐	☑	☐	☐	☑	☐	☐	☐	☐	☐	☑	☐	R6	9
R7	☑	☐	☐	☐	☐	☐	☐	☐	☑	☐	☐	☐	☐	☐	☑	☑	☐	☐	☐	☐	☐	☐	☑	☐	☐	R7	1
R8	☑	☐	☐	☐	☐	☐	☑	☐	☐	☐	☐	☐	☐	☐	☑	☐	☐	☑	☐	☐	☐	☐	☐	☑	☐	R8	3
R9	☐	☐	☑	☐	☐	☐	☑	☐	☐	☐	☐	☐	☐	☑	☐	☐	☑	☐	☐	☐	☐	☐	☐	☑	☐	R9	8
R10	☐	☐	☐	☑	☐	☐	☐	☐	☑	☐	☐	☐	☐	☑	☐	☐	☐	☐	☑	☐	☐	☑	☐	☐	☐	R10	10

Elicitation of stakeholder's initial preferences — Lowest to highest preference value

Matching and Selection Process

This requirement recommendation process is initiated using a tool support where top 3 ranked requirements obtained from stakeholder's are entered along with their priority preference values (refer figure 2). Knowledge extraction of similar requirement(s) matching stakeholder interest is performed on data and meta-data stored in central repository maintained over a hybrid cloud. From this requirement repository requirements similar matching requirements criteria are retrieved, modified to tune it according to the need of the current project and are subsequently stored in repository for future use. A hybrid cloud deployment model is used as a main database and is shared by various organizations supporting the concept of reusability. The involvement of organizations will help increasing the requirement gathering coverage domain for better reusability. Hybrid cloud allows one to extend either the capacity of a cloud service, by aggregation, integration or customization with another cloud service (Mell & Grance, 2011) for providing data security through public and private cloud services. This study uses heroku cloud platform (Heroku).

Stakeholder's enter initial product requirements along with ranking of importance for each. The whole process of matching is divided into two levels: goal base (representing data part of requirement) which stores details pertaining to domain and functionality of each requirement expressed as requirement tuple and deep analysis base (representing metadata and relationship part of requirement) which stores details pertaining to their probable effort, risk and correlation among requirements. Staged information extraction and matching will build the confidence of progression

Figure 2. Snapshot to enter top 3 ranked requirements obtained from stakeholder's.

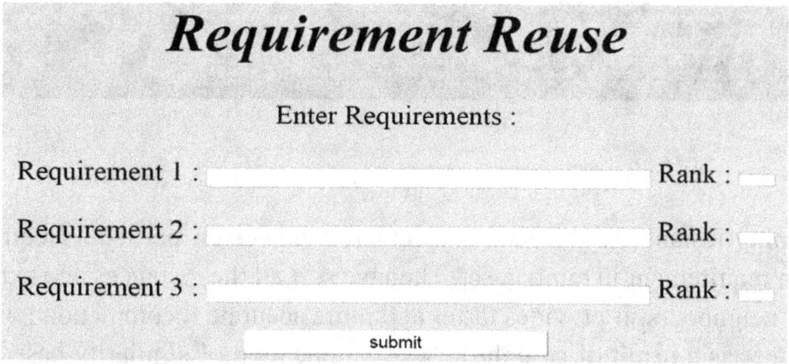

towards desirable requirements for reuse. Proposed intersective way (i-way) method, uses intersection of results of two machine learning algorithm namely, K-nearest neighbours (KNN) and term frequency–inverse document frequency (TF-IDF). i-way is a 2-level extraction framework which represents win-win situation by considering intersective results of two different approaches to ensure that selection is progressing towards desired requirement for reuse consideration. Firstly, it utilizes a content based recommender, based on kNN algorithm to generate recommendations. Secondly, it utilizes cosine similarity scores method to find most similar requirement from the initial input. This recommendation tool supports searching, selecting, modify and update operations.

Validation and Results Observation

To perform validation and observe promising results, we have applied proposed approach on a sample case study similar to dataset (Shaukat et al., 2014) so that matching requirements of interest can be selected for reuse. Figure 3, 4 and 5 represents the results obtained for recommendation.

A positive integer k (number of recommendations) is specified along with the initial requirement of the project. We select the k entries in our dataset which are closest to our initial requirement. We make these predictions just-in-time by calculating the similarity between an input sample and each training instance. In

Figure 3. Recommendations with KNN

Figure 4. Recommendations with Cosine Similarity

Requirements	project category	Requirement category	Magnitude of Risk	Impact	Priority
The system shall allow user to update the profile information	Transaction Processing System	Functional	Medium	moderate	34.4
The system shall allow user to update the profile information.	Transaction Processing System	Functional	Very High	moderate	36.607692
The system shall allow user to create profile and set his credential	Transaction Processing System	Functional	Medium	Low	42.376923
The system shall allow user to create profile and set his credential.	Transaction Processing System	Functional	Low	Low	25.469231
The system shall authenticate user credentials to view the profile	Transaction Processing System	Functional	Low	Low	25.630769

each training instance, a distance is calculated between a particular requirement with each requirement in our dataset. Then we sort all the distances and extract the k nearest neighbours. It provides faster and more accurate recommendations to the stakeholders as a result of straight forward application of similarity based on the distance for the purpose of classification.

For cosine similarity based recommendation (Figure 4) we start by creating a dictionary of words (i.e. bag of words) present in the whole document space. We ignore commonly occurring words also called as stop words as these words will not help in choosing the relevant words. Given the dictionary of all such terms T = {t1, t2, . . ., tn}, each requirement in dataset, ri is represented as a vector of terms, vi = (ri,1, ri,2, . . ., ri,n) where ri,j is a term weight representing the number of occurrences of term tj in requirement ri. These term weights are then transformed using a standard term-frequency, inverse document frequency (tf-idf) approach such that, tf -idf(ri,j) = ri,j $\bullet$ log2(D/drj) where D represents the total number of requirements, and drj represents the number of requirements containing term tj . Finally, the transformed vector (with tf-idf weights) is normalized to a unit vector resulting in the vector Vi = (Ri,1, Ri,2, . . ., Ri,n). Cosine similarity is a measure of similarity between two nonzero vectors. How closely two sentences are related are based on the angle their respective vector makes. So if two vectors make an angle 0 degree, then cosine value would be 1, which would mean that the sentences are closely related to each other. Similarity scores for all requirements in dataset is then sorted and top n requirements are displayed where n can be 1<=n<=D. Taking the intersections of recommendation of both the algorithms will be the requirements which will be highly recommended to the stakeholders (Figure 5).

Hence it can be concluded that the proposed approach can help in effective requirement gathering and can save cost, time, effort and communication problems involved in requirement gathering.

Figure 5. Final Recommendations using i-way

Requirements	project category	Requirement category	Magnitude of Risk	Impact	Priority
The system shall allow user to create profile and set his credential.	Transaction Processing System	Functional	Low	Low	25.469231
The system shall authenticate user credentials to view the profile	Transaction Processing System	Functional	Low	Low	25.630769

CONCLUSION

This paper presents a novel i-way approach for mining and recommending project specific requirements for reusability. To achieve this, this paper has introduced an intersective algorithm (i-way), which gives recommendations by using intersection of two algorithms KNN and Tf-Idf Cosine Similarity. Recommendations are made after gathering (explicitly or implicitly), analyzing user or the details of the project and processing the details of all the projects with the algorithms to recommend the requirements more accurately. Moreover, we have also introduced a new Ranking feature which helps to understand the need of the user in a better way and give more accurate recommendations.

REFERENCES

Ali, N. B., Petersen, K., & Wohlin, C. (2014). A systematic literature review on the industrial use of software process simulation. *Journal of Systems and Software, 97,* 65–85. doi:10.1016/j.jss.2014.06.059

Bakar, N. H., Kasirun, Z. M., & Salleh, N. (2015). Terms Extractions: An Approach for Requirements Reuse. In *2nd International Conference on Information Science and Security (ICISS)* (pp. 1-4). Seoul, South Korea: IEEE. 10.1109/ICISSEC.2015.7371034

Bellinzona, R., Fugini, M. G., & de Mey, V. (1993). *Reuse of specifications and designs in a development information system. In Information System Development Process* (pp. 79–96). Amsterdam: North-Holland. doi:10.1016/B978-0-444-81594-1.50011-8

Bellinzona, R., Fugini, M. G., & Pernici, B. (1992). *An environment for specification reuse. Technical Report POLIMIUDUNIV.92.E.2.9E.8.4.* ITHACA.

Benitti, F. B. V., & da Silva, R. C. (2013). Evaluation of a systematic approach to requirements reuse. *Journal of Universal Computer Science, 19*(2), 254–280.

Castro-Herrera, C., Duan, C., Cleland-Huang, J., & Mobasher, B. (2008). Using data mining and recommender systems to facilitate large-scale, open, and inclusive requirements elicitation processes. In *16th IEEE International Requirements Engineering Conference.* Catalunya, Spain: IEEE. 10.1109/RE.2008.47

Chou, S. C., Chen, J. Y., & Chung, C. G. (1996). A behaviour based classification and retrieval technique for object-oriented software reuse. *Proceedings of the Journal of Software Practice and Experience*, *26*(7), 815–832. doi:10.1002/(SICI)1097-024X(199607)26:7<815::AID-SPE32>3.0.CO;2-#

Cybulski, J. L. (1998). *Patterns in software requirements reuse. Technical report, Department of Information Systems*. University of Melbourne.

Elberzhager, F., Rosbach, A., Münch, J., & Eschbach, R. (2012). Reducing test effort: A systematic mapping study on existing approaches. *Information and Software Technology*, *54*(10), 1092–1106. doi:10.1016/j.infsof.2012.04.007

Eriksson, M., Börstler, J., & Borg, K. (2009). Managing requirements specifications for product lines - An approach and industry case study. *Journal of Systems and Software*, *82*(3), 435–447. doi:10.1016/j.jss.2008.07.046

Goldin, L., & Berry, D. M. (2015). Reuse of requirements reduced time to market at one industrial shop: A case study. *Requirements Engineering*, *20*(1), 23–44. doi:10.100700766-013-0182-7

Heroku platform, https://www.heroku.com/

Hwang, C. L., & Yoon, K. P. (1981). *Multiple attributes decision making methods and applications*. Berlin: Springer-Verlag. doi:10.1007/978-3-642-48318-9

Ivarsson, M., & Gorschek, T. (2011). A method for evaluating rigor and industrial relevance of technology evaluations. *Empirical Software Engineering*, *16*(3), 365–395. doi:10.100710664-010-9146-4

Kotonya, G., & Sommerville, I. (1997). *Requeriments Engineering: Processes Techniques*. Wiley.

Lamsweerde, A. V. (2000). Requirements engineering in the year 00: A research perspective. In *Proceedings of 22nd International Conference on Software Engineering* (pp. 5-19). Limerich: ACM Press. 10.1145/337180.337184

Lim, S., & Finkelstein, A. (2012). Using social networks and collaborative filtering for large-scale requirement elicitation. *IEEE Transactions on Software Engineering*, *38*(3), 707–735. doi:10.1109/TSE.2011.36

Maalej, W., & Thuremella, A. (2009). Towards a Research Agenda for Recommendation Systems in Requirements Engineering. In *Second International Workshop on Managing Requirements Knowledge (MaRK'09)*. Atlanta, GA: IEEE. 10.1109/MARK.2009.12

Maiden, N., & Sutcliffe, A. (1992). Exploiting reusable specifications through anology. Proceedings of Magazine-. *Communications of the ACM, 35*(4), 55–64. doi:10.1145/129852.129857

Mannion, M., Kaindl, H. J., Wheaton, & Keepence, B. (1999). Reusing single system requirements from Application family requirements. In *Proceedings of the 21st international conference on software engineering* (pp. 453-462). Los Angeles, CA: Academic Press.

Mell, P., & Grance, T. (2011). *The NIST definition of cloud computing.* Academic Press.

Mobasher, B., & Cleland-Huang, J. (2009). Recommender systems in requirements engineering. In *Second International Workshop.* Chicago: DePaul University.

Moon, M., Yeom, K., & Chae, H. S. (2005). An approach to developing domain requirements as a core asset based on commonality and variability analysis in Software Engineering. *IEEE Transactions on Software Engineering, 31*(7), 551–569. doi:10.1109/TSE.2005.76

Munir, H., Moayyed, M., & Petersen, K. (2014). Considering rigor and relevance when evaluating test driven development: A systematic review. *Information and Software Technology, 56*(4), 375–394. doi:10.1016/j.infsof.2014.01.002

Munir, H., Wnuk, K., & Runeson, P. (2016). Open innovation in software engineering: A systematic mapping study. *Empirical Software Engineering, 21*(2), 684–723. doi:10.100710664-015-9380-x

Pacheco, C., Garcia, I., Calvo-Manzano, J. A., & Arcilla, M. (2017). Reusing functional software requirements in small-sized software enterprises: A model oriented to the catalog of requirements. *Requirements Engineering, 22*(2), 275–287. doi:10.100700766-015-0243-1

Pacheco, C. L., Garcia, I. A., Calvo Manzano, J. A., & Arcilla, M. (2015). A proposed model for reuse of software requirements in requirements catalog. *Journal of Software: Evolution and Process, 27*(1), 1–21. doi:10.3156/jsoft.27.1_1

Paydar, S., & Kahani, M. (2015). A semantic web enabled approach to reuse functional requirements models in web engineering. *Automated Software Engineering, 22*(2), 241–288. doi:10.100710515-014-0144-4

Schmitt, C., & Liggesmeyer, P. (2015). A Model for Structuring and Reusing Security Requirements Sources and Security Requirements. In REFSQ Workshops, Vancouver, Canada.

Shaukat, Z., Naseem, R., & Zubair, M. (2018). *Software Requirement Risk Prediction Dataset*. Retrieved from https://zenodo.org/record/1209601#.XJsL_JgzaM-

Sutcliffe, A., Maiden, N., Minocha, S., & Manuel, D. (1998). Supporting scenario-based requirements engineering. *IEEE Transactions on Software Engineering*, *24*(12), 1072–1088. doi:10.1109/32.738340

Woo, H. G., & Robinson, W. N. (2002). Reuse of scenario specifications using an automated relational learner a lightweight approach. In *Proceedings of Joint International Conference on Requirements Engineering*. Essen, Germany: IEEE. 10.1109/ICRE.2002.1048520

Chapter 3

Requirement–Based Test Approach and Traceability for High–Integrity Airborne Embedded Systems

Sudha Srinivasan
Aeronautical Development Agency (ADA), Bangalore, India

D. S. Chauhan
GLA University Mathura, Mathura, India

ABSTRACT

One of the biggest challenges in the development of airborne embedded systems is to ensure that the aircraft subsystem meets all its user specifications and ascertain that no important functionality is missing which leads to development of an incorrect product. This chapter proposes a methodology for achieving requirement traceability and thereby performing requirement-based testing for efficient test and evaluation of aircraft subsystems. This methodology integrates requirement traceability throughout the software development life cycle along with requirement-based testing for high-integrity software systems. The methodology has been found to be most effective in revealing errors and optimizes testing by preventing repetition of test cases across test platforms. This unique contribution has the potential to revolutionize the research world in software engineering.

DOI: 10.4018/978-1-5225-9659-2.ch003

INTRODUCTION

A well-defined software development process is essential for realization of highly reliable and safe software with cost and utilization benefits during the entire life cycle.

The software used in airborne embedded systems runs to several million lines of code and complete testing of this humongous software is a significant challenge. The process essential for certifying this airborne embedded software involves a number of software lifecycle documents where requirement traceability is essential for the entire cycle starting from capturing of system requirements to testing.

Research has shown that requirement traceability is an important contributing factor to software project failures and budget overruns. Requirements traceability refers to the ability to describe and follow the life of a requirement, in both forward and backward direction (i.e., from its origins, through its development and specification, to its subsequent deployment and use, and through periods of on-going refinement and iteration in any of these phases) (Gotel & Finkelstein, 1994).

Traceability makes it easy to determine what requirements, design, code, and test cases need to be updated to fulfil a change request made during the software project's development and maintenance phase and also to analyze the impact of a requirement change. Traceability links among the software development life cycle artefacts brings out how a software system was implemented to accommodate its requirements.

Many standards have been adopted in aircraft subsystems for software development like U.S.Department of Defense (DoD) standard 2167A (U.S. Department of Defense, 1988) which mandates requirement traceability.

In the conventional approach to testing, the traceability of requirements to test cases is carried out only during system testing which occurs late in the development life cycle and the resulting observations lead to large amount of rework. Thus making testing the costliest method of finding bugs.

Also, during the development of complex high integrity airborne embedded systems, there is frequent change in requirements leading to rework in design, code and testing leading to large project delays and cost implications.

Requirement based testing is a solution to these problems identified and is the suggested approach that focuses on integrating requirements with testing throughout the software development life cycle and avoids repetition of test cases across life cycle phases.

The strategy of requirement based testing is emphasized in the DO-178B guideline adopted by the aerospace industry.

In this paper, we first elaborate the observed problems in the current approach of requirement traceability and software system testing and then propose a methodology to address the challenges. The methodology optimizes software testing which addresses major issues of validating the necessary and sufficient set of test cases from requirements to ensure that the design and code fully meet those requirements. This approach saves time and cost by avoiding repetition of tests across platforms.

This paper integrates requirement traceability throughout the software development lifecycle along with the requirement based testing for high integrity software systems.

BACKGROUND

B. Ramesh, T. Powers, C. Stubbs and M. Edwards 1995, presented a case study that suggested implementing traceability into the organization's systems development methodology as "an important concept in improving the process of systems engineering activity and overall project quality." The paper details a case study focussed on the use of requirement traceability starting from the system requirements down to the computer software unit (CSU) level. Once the project reaches the testing phase, this traceability is used to prove that the system meets the stated requirements (Ramesh, Powers, Stubbs, & Edwards, 1995).

Jane Cleland-Huang, 2006 addressed the problems and challenges of requirement traceability along with the traditional and automated methods. The open question on what kind of traceability is used to achieve the desired results in a cost effective way is addressed (Cleland-Huang, 2006).

PredragSkoković and MarijaRakić-Skoković, 2010 have described the requirement based test methodology as a 12 step process for verifying the code against test cases. The paper discusses the introduction of requirement based testing before the implementation phase (Predrag, Skokovic, & Rakic-Skokovis, 2010).

Muhammad Shahid, Suhaimi Ibrahim, and MohdNaz'riMahrin, (2011) evaluated eleven requirements management and traceability tools and compared some of their features including tools category, different functionalities of tools and their empirical evidence. The paper has listed requirement management tools as well as pure traceability tools (Shahid, Ibrahim, & Mahrin, 2011).

Soo Min Ooi, Raymond Lim and Chee Cheng Lim, 2014 proposed an integrated solution, which links requirement development and management tool with test management system to achieve end -to-end traceability. This approach focuses on establishment of traceability from requirements to test coverage (Ooi, Lim, & Lim, 2014).

John Lee and Jon Friedman 2013 have described how cause effect graphs can be applied in simulink models to achieve requirement model coverage in their paper on requirement modelling and automated requirement based test generation.[10]

There has been significant work in the area of requirement traceability and the concept of requirement based testing as described in the above papers which form the base for this paper.

However, the approach described in this paper proposes the following aspects that are not covered in any of the above papers:

- Bottom Up approach to testing: Commence testing at system integration level rather than CSU level.
- Achieve traceability from software high level and low level requirements to system integration test cases.
- Avoid repetition of test cases across test platforms namely CSU level tests and System integration level tests.
- Achieve 100% functional and a large percentage of structural coverage during system integration testing.
- Minimize the effort of module / CSU level testing that is a cumbersome process.
- Accomplish Cost effective testing for airborne embedded systems that has a high rate of new/changing requirements.

CURRENT METHODS FOR REQUIREMENT TRACEABILITY AND TESTING PROCESS

The software artefacts generated during the software development life cycle for airborne high integrity software systems includes the System/Subsystem Specifications (SSS) which bifurcates the hardware and software requirements of the system, Software Requirement Specifications (SRS), Software Design Document (SDD), Source Code, Software Test Description & Report (STDR) for module level testing and Software Test Description & Report (STDR) for Software System Testing. The DOD-STD-2167A (Whalen, Rajan, Heimdahl, & Miller, 2006) is one of the standards followed for software development and testing.

Traceability is achieved manually and documented in all the artefacts by providing unique numbering for requirements in SSS & SRS, design functions in SDD, Block of lines in source code and test cases in STDR.

In airborne software systems the strategy of testing includes the Module level testing for achieving structural coverage followed by the software system testing for achieving functional coverage. Test planning tasks encompass different types of testing—module level test, software integration test, and software system test. The planning activities result in documentation for each test type consisting of Software test plan and Software test description & report documents.

Figure 1. Traceability and Testing

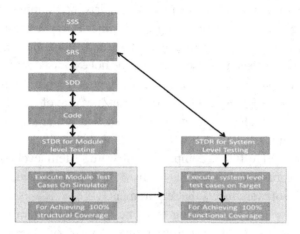

Figure 1 shows the traceability to be manually shown across the software life cycle artifacts and the sequence of testing activities to be carried out across the software development life cycle.

The testing process followed currently involves module level testing that verifies a module's logic, computations, functionality, and error handling. Further, the software integration test activity is performed to examine how modules interface and interact with each other. Tool is used which instruments the code that is executed on the simulator.

For module level testing and Software integration testing, IBM Rational Test Real Time has been used to test on simulator. A typical global coverage graph obtained using the tool is shown in figure 2.

Figure 2. Coverage Graph

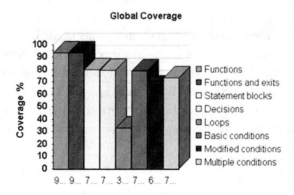

In module level testing, the logic of individual subprograms, subroutines or procedures in the code is analysed by providing a driver for supplying the test data, monitoring the execution and capturing the results. Here, structural coverage of software is ensured in terms of coverage like statement coverage, decision coverage etc.

Code coverage analysis finds the lines of code not exercised by a set of test cases thus creating additional test cases to increase coverage and determining a quantitative measure of code coverage, which is an important measure of quality.

However, it is difficult to write good unit tests and for large complex software, entire process is cumbersome and time consuming.

Once module level testing is completed, software system level testing is carried out on the target hardware. It is critical to ensure that the interfaces are correct, and that the resulting software meets the requirements.

The Software system level testing examines what the program accomplishes, without regard to how it works internally and compares the program behaviour against a requirements specification.

Test cases are prepared for each requirement stated in the SRS and executed on the target hardware in order to achieve 100% functional coverage. Testing is carried out on the target using an integrated test facility comprising of all the hardware interfaces to the unit under test.

In a nutshell, the current method includes traceability being achieved manually which is time consuming and cumbersome. The testing process involves repetition of tests during structural and functional testing thereby increasing effort and time. Figure 3 shows the testing approach and sequence in module level testing and system level testing processes. The two testing processes are independent of one another thereby resulting in repetition of tests across platforms.

RESEARCH CHALLENGES

Requirement traceability in aircraft subsystems is an important aspect to comply with. This traceability as described in section 3 of this paper, is shown by manually mapping the requirements in the SSS to requirements in SRS, requirements in the SRS to the functions/modules in the design document (SDD), functions/modules in (SDD) to source code, lines in code to the module level test cases in the STDR and lastly the requirements in SSS and SRS to the test cases in the STDR of Software system testing. There is a high possibility of erroneous mappings due the manual nature of achieving requirement traceability of the software artefacts which is one of the challenges.

Figure 3. Current Test Approach

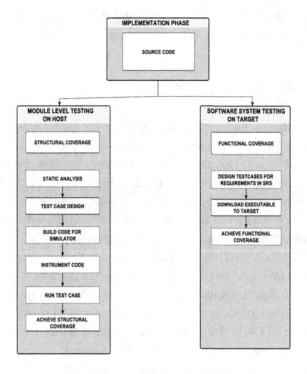

The module level testing of one sample sub system of the weapon management system of the aircraft comprising of approximately 40,000 lines of code involved execution of 600 module level test cases on the host system for achieving structural code coverage without considering the functional aspects.

The structural code coverage of 100% for Modified Condition Decision Coverage (MCDC) was achieved during host testing using RTRT test tool. In MC/DC analysis, a boolean decision consists of multiple boolean conditions such that every condition shall be evaluated to true and false and it is required that this switch changes the outcome of the final decision. Further, this code was again subjected to software system testing against the requirements without considering the internal code structure and 1250 test cases were executed on the target environment. Here, the functional coverage of requirements was achieved. There was no link between the above two activities resulting in a significant repetition of test cases in the two phases of testing thereby increasing the effort, cost and time. Testing thoroughly within the given time schedule is another challenging aspect. In order to address these challenges, the philosophy of requirement based test approach with traceability is being proposed.

Requirements-based tests are function tests. This process addresses two major issues: first, verify that all requirements are testable and second, design a necessary and sufficient set of test cases from those requirements (Whalen et al, 2006).

PROPOSED METHODOLOGY

This paper describes a tool based methodology evolved for the upstream and downstream tracing of requirements throughout the software life cycle so that traceability is established. This also proves to be very important for impact analysis during the maintenance phase of the aircraft subsystem. Once the traceability is established, requirement based testing is carried out by using the LDRA tool that provides automation which can be effectively used to reduce effort, time and cost.

Following traceability activities have been carried out:

Requirements in the SSS is traced to requirements in SRS, high level requirements in SRS is traced to low level requirements in the design document (SDD), low level requirements in the design document (SDD) are traced to the functions/modules in code, low level requirements in the design document (SDD) are finally traced to the test cases in the STDR of Software system testing. Further, the upstream tracing has also been carried out back to the source requirements.

Automation of bi-directional requirement traceability has been achieved by using the LDRA test tool whose capabilities include traceability and test management. Regular Expressions are written to extract the unique Identifier that can be used to establish traceability across life cycle documents. The regular expression library was used to check if a string matches a specified pattern as a whole, and search within a string for a substring atching as a specified pattern. The proposed approach is depicted in the following figure 4:

Figure 4. Proposed Approach

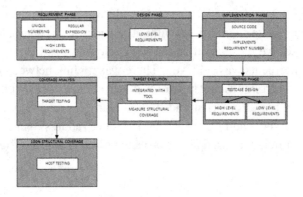

The detailed workflow for this methodology is as follows:

a)   Ensure Unique Numbering in all life cycle artifacts

Most of the requirements/documentation for aircraft subsystems have been written using Microsoft Word where the style of the unique identifiers is used to trace across documents.

A style **is** a set of formatting characteristics that you can apply to text in your document to quickly change their appearance. When you apply a style, you apply a whole group of formats in one simple task. Some examples of style are Normal, Heading 1, Heading 2 etc. The software life cycle artifacts of the aircraft subsystems namely SSS, SRS, SDD and STDR are all documented using MS Word. All the documents need to be uniquely numbered. Thus, for the artifacts documented using MS Word, unique numbering with a predefined style is ensured.

In code, words like "Implements", "Covers" is prefixed with a unique number and added as comment in the appropriate segment of the code.

For example: /* Implements PI-5012

b)   Regular Expressions

The requirements are imported from MS word using regular expressions.To capture the requirements, we use regular expressions which could depend on the style of the text. As shown below we can see the pattern captured under group1.

Regular Expression used → ^Heading 2\t.*(SSS_PIB_PI-\d\d\d\d)

Text inside the bracket marks the group that acts as the capturing element for the regular expression. Tracing is performed with a text starting from Heading followed by a space, a digit (2 here), and tab character followed by any number of characters containing the Group.

Figure 5 shows the unique numbering of requirements captured using regular expressions.

c)   Mapping of software life cycle artifacts

The mapping of high level requirements with low level requirements (design) and further the mapping of low level requirements with source code procedures is carried out. The traceability between Source Code and low-level requirements enables verification of the absence of undocumented Source Code and verification of the complete implementation of low-level requirements.

Figure 5. Unique Numbering of requirements

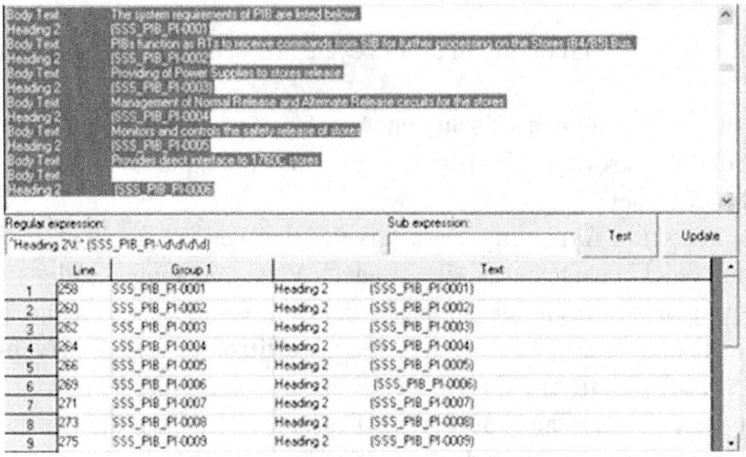

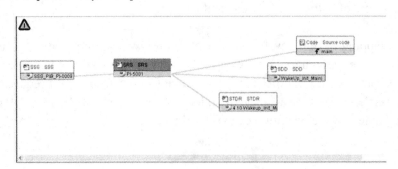

These mapped requirements are subsequently made available to the tester for the creation of test cases for achieving functional coverage. The results of this workflow is then be mapped back to the requirements sources.

d)   Impact Analysis

As requirements are traced to design and then to code and later to test cases, it is possible to estimate the project completion status based on how many requirements have been traced to artifacts created later in the development cycle. This information can be used to estimate the schedule for a project during development and can be used to assess risk and the impact.

The impact analysis report is generated in graphical form as shown in figure 6 using the tool.

Figure 6. Impact Analysis Report

e)   Requirement Based Testing on target

Once the requirement traceability is obtained, the requirements are assigned to test engineers by project manager using the tool in order to carry out requirement based testing.

Now, Requirement based testing (RBT) focuses on the compliance of the software with the requirements and structural coverage focuses on testing the source code structurally to ensure that there is no unnecessary code in the implementation.

For RBT, the most important criteria is to analyse and ensure that every functional requirement of the system as specified in the SSS is well documented in the SRS (High level requirements) and SDD (Low level requirements) . Further, the test cases in the STDR should be traceable to these high level as well as low level requirements. The test cases are designed for covering each of the low level requirements which also ensures that code structures meeting the low level requirements are covered.

The tool is integrated with the test setup used for system integration testing .This tool based methodology not only covers the requirements tested for functionality but also indicates the code structure that is covered during this testing by providing structural coverage statistics.

This way we largely reduce the labour intensive process of writing module level test cases thereby achieving both structural as well as functional coverage with a common set of test cases thus reducing time and cost.

The instrumented code is executed on the target and the results are analysed. Figure 7 shows the partial coverage achieved by carrying out the system integration testing on target.

RBT is carried out, on the target by integrating with the test tool. Hence, test coverage analysis provides both structural coverage as well as requirement based test coverage.

Figure 7. Partial Coverage

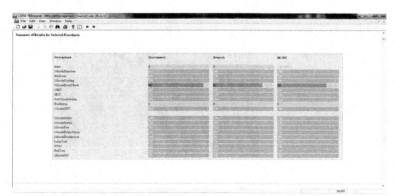

f)   Achieving Complete Structural Coverage

After carrying out the System Integration Testing on target, coverage results are analysed. If the software functionality is covered and yet there is presence of uncovered code, then this needs to be first analysed to determine and reason out whether the requirements are inadequate, test cases are inadequate or dead code is present.

If software requirements are inadequate, then SRS is updated and associated test cases are designed and executed on the target. If there is missing coverage of requirements, test cases are modified to provide the missing coverage, Dead code, if present is to be removed.

There exists one more reason for achieving reduced coverage especially at the RBT carried out during System Integration Testing of airborne embedded systems. This could be due to the limitation of the system integration test facility. Upgrading the test facility software/hardware in order to overcome this limitation may not be practically possible.

This is when module level/CSU level tests are carried out by adding test cases to cater to the required structural coverage. Figure 8 shows the Complete coverage achieved by carrying out the tool based structural coverage.

The additional test cases required to achieve the above coverage results is shown below in figure 9. These test cases could not be executed on the target during system integration testing due to the limitation of the aircraft level system integration test facility. As seen, the module level testing effort on host has been largely reduced in order to execute only a small number of test cases required to achieve complete structural coverage. This has in turn reduced the time and cost.

Figure 8. Complete Coverage

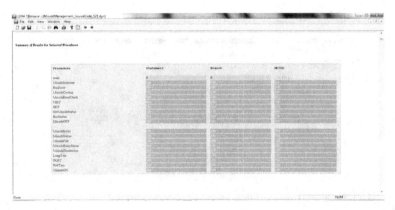

Figure 9. Additional Test Cases

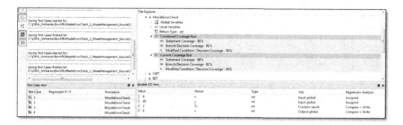

g)   Achieving End to End Traceability

Once the requirement based testing on target is completed, the traceability across the software development life cycle is viewed and reported, the traceability from the SSS to requirements in SRS, high level requirements in the SRS to the low level requirements in the design document (SDD) and further SDD to source code as shown in figure 10. The traceability of low level requirements to test cases is shown in figure 11. The figures clearly depict the end to end traceability achieved from requirements to test cases. Requirement traceability across the development and testing process is a measure of software quality and is achieved using this methodology. The test coverage metrics is integrated with the requirements thereby improving the effort and test efficiency.

Figure 10. Traceability across life cycle artifacts

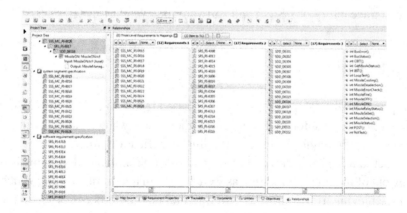

Figure 11. Traceability of low level requirements to Test Cases

FUTURE RESEARCH DIRECTIONS

Future work in this area can be Model centric approach for Requirement handover from system to software, mapping of system models to software models and model based test case design.

The model based system engineering uses models as an integral part of the technical baseline and formalizes the system development from concept phase to operations thus enabling analysis of system design before it is built. The integration of Model based system engineering with model based software engineering and requirement based testing of the models is the future challenge that will have an increased ability to manage system complexity. This involves the migration from document centric to model centric, from system models to software models, and requirement based testing of the models followed by auto code generation which will also require integration of multiple system engineering and software engineering tools to achieve complete end to end traceability of system and software life cycle artifacts.

CONCLUSION

The proposed methodology of requirement based test with traceability is found to be efficient especially for high integrity airborne software systems owing to the frequent change in requirements and minimal certification time.

The methodology currently followed for airborne embedded systems involves carrying out of module level testing as well as system integration testing which may result in achieving 100% coverage after a cumbersome process of testing across multiple platforms .

Compared to the current methodology, the proposed approach in this paper has been found to effectively reduce development cost, effort and time and also facilitates early detection and correction of errors.

It is observed that the number of test cases executed in order to achieve 100% structural and functional coverage reduces by 50%. Also, as described in the paper there is no repetition of test cases across platforms in the proposed methodology. The proposed methodology is highly recommended and can be effectively followed for airborne embedded systems.

REFERENCES

Cleland-Huang, J. (2006). Just Enough Requirements Traceability. In *Proceedings of the 30th Annual International Computer Software and Applications Conference (COMPSAC'06)*. Chicago, IL: IEEE. 10.1109/COMPSAC.2006.57

Gotel, O., & Finkelstein, C. W. (1994). An Analysis of the Requirements Traceability Problem. In *Proceedings of First International Conference on Requirements Engineering* (p94-121). Colorado Springs, CO: IEEE. 10.1109/ICRE.1994.292398

Lee & Friedman. (2013). *Requirements Modeling and Automated Requirements-Based Test Generation*. Paper presented at SAE 2013 AeroTech Congress & Exhibition, Montreal, Canada.

Ooi, S. M., Lim, R., & Lim, C. C. (2014). An Integrated System for End-To-End Traceability and Requirements Test Coverage. In *Proceedings of IEEE 5th International Conference on Software Engineering and Service Science*. Beijing, China: IEEE. 10.1109/ICSESS.2014.6933511

Predrag, S., & Marija, R.-S. (2010). Requirements-Based Testing Process in Practice. *International Journal of Industrial Engineering and Management, 1*(4), 155–161.

Ramesh, B., Powers, T., Stubbs, C., & Edwards, M. (1995). Implementing Requirements Traceability: A Case Study, In *Proceedings of IEEE International Symposium on Requirements Engineering (RE'95)*. York, UK: IEEE. 10.1109/ISRE.1995.512549

RTCA-DO-178B. (1992). *Software Considerations in Airborne Systems and Equipment Certification*. RTCA SC-167 / EUROCAE WG-12.USA:RTCA.

Shahid, Ibrahim, & Mahrin. (2011). An Evaluation of Requirements Management and Traceability Tool. *International Journal of Computer, Electrical, Automation, Control and Information Engineering, 5*(6).

U.S. Department of Defense. (1988). *Defense systems software development, DODSTD- 2167A, Military standard*. US DOD.

Whalen, M., Rajan, A., Heimdahl, M., & Miller, S. (2006). Coverage metrics for requirements-based testing. In *Proceedings of International Symposium on Software Testing and Analysis, ISSTA* (p 25–36). Portland, ME: ISSTA.

Chapter 4

A Systematic Literature Review on Risk Assessment and Mitigation Approaches in Requirement Engineering

Priyanka Chandani
Jaypee Institute of Information Technology, Noida, India

Chetna Gupta
Jaypee Institute of Information Technology, Noida, India

ABSTRACT

Risk assessment and management practice is an organized way to identify, analyze, and assess the impacts of risks and mitigate them when they arise. Risk can occur in any phase of software development and is a significant step for better supervision of threats. The purpose of this study is to identify and analyze existing risk assessment and management techniques from a historical perspective that address and study risk management and perception of risk. The chapter presents extensive summary of existing literature on various techniques and approaches related to requirements defects, defect taxonomy, its classification, and its potential impact on software development as the main contributions of this research work. The primary objective of this study was to present a systematic literature review of techniques/methods/ tools for risk assessment and management. This research successfully identifies and discovers existing risk assessment and management techniques, their limitations, taxonomies, processes, and identifies possible improvements for better defect identification and prevention.

DOI: 10.4018/978-1-5225-9659-2.ch004

BACKGROUND, MOTIVATION AND INTRODUCTION

The software industry is going through a revolution at a rapid pace where both business and technology domains are evolving very fast. This time-to-deliver market puts pressure on software development teams to deliver quality software well in time which establishes the need for performing rigorous risk analysis (Arshad, 2007). Studies have shown that inappropriate and misleading requirement gathering is the most expensive and are one of the fundamental drivers of project failures (Glass, 1998). As reported by (Pohl & Rupp, 2010), 60% of project venture disappointments fall into requirements engineering phase and generally aren't found until late in development life cycle or when the project has gone live (Boehm, 1981). The same facts are supported by (Lindquist, 2005) which conclude that *"poor requirements management can be attributed to 71% of software projects that fail; greater than bad technology missed deadlines, and change management issues"*. Therefore, one of the significant challenges in requirements engineering is to have legible requirements, which are free from unknowns and failures. Any failures during RE phase have an adverse impact on the overall development process (Hall, Beecham & Rainer, 2002) as it acts as a roadmap for calculating schedule and cost of the system under development.

Risk assessment and management is a sub disciple of software engineering which in an organized way identifies, analyze and assess the impacts of risks and mitigate them when they arise. Risk can occur in any phase of software lifecycle due to the scope of an assortment of potential problems that can emerge in different levels of software development. To have confidence in fulfilling product roadmap and complete release based on their timeline, the risk has to be eliminated as early as possible (Rabia & Muhammad, 2013). It is one of the overlooked aspects in requirements engineering (Stern & Arias, 2011) and is generally considered as a potential problem that can negatively affect the projects. However, risk can also have a positive effect in terms of opportunities. As per guide to the Project Management Body of Knowledge (PMBOK), *"project risk is an uncertain event or condition, that, if occurs, has a positive or a negative effect on a project objective"* (2017). Conventional risk management process as exercised by a larger part of project managers tend to focus on risk by spending considerable effort on identifying and managing threats, ignoring positive side of risk (Hillson, 2002). According to (McConnell, 1997), risk management requires 5% of the aggregate project budget to get a 50–70% possibility of staying away from time to avoid overrun. Researchers in the past have proposed a considerable amount of risk identification, analysis, and management models, for better supervision of threats (Guiling & Xiaojuan, 2011).

This chapter aims to provide a critical review of the studies conducted by researchers in the past focusing mainly in the area of software risk assessment at requirement engineering phase of SDLC. The scope of the survey is to find out assessment tools and methods there are available, what results they produce and risk management process as a whole. The research community will be able to use this literature study as a starting point for further research.

The chapter is structured as follows: first, the details about the systematic review process are given and discussed. The studies related to risk management models are briefly discussed along with the current practices of risk assessment and mapping of the models on different life cycle stages to give a complete view on risk management. Finally, the current state of the art is summarized followed by the conclusion.

RESEARCH METHOD

This study has been undertaken as a complete literature review based on the work done by various researchers in the risk assessment and management field. In this case, the goal of the review is to assess the literature available on the subject of discussion. Steps in this complete literature review method involve the selection of sources and search process as depicted below in Figure 1:

Source Selection

The following resources were explored to mine relevant data resources to conduct this review work: IEEE Xplore, ACM Digital Library, ScienceDirect, Web of Science, Springer, Google Scholar, and other databases. In addition to search results returned by popular databases, an intensive manual search on title, abstract and index term was conducted to accumulate research work of different dimensions for analysis. For in-depth analysis, reference lists of shortlisted papers were inspected for additional relevant papers.

Search Process

More analysis was necessary to streamline these studies to relevant ones. First, the title of each study and their contents were briefly studied. Hence, all the papers that do not address the topic of discussion were excluded from the relevant studies list. Also, only studies are written and published in the english language from journals, conference proceedings, workshops, symposiums, book chapters, and relevant technical articles were considered for inclusion in the list of relevant studies. The duplicate and ambiguous papers are removed from the list. Specifically, we performed

Figure 1. Complete Literature Review Process

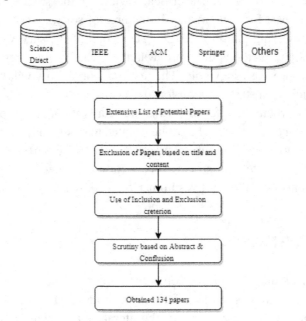

a complete literature review for risk assessment and management on articles published since 1986. Table 1 shows the inclusion and exclusion criteria for selecting primary studies and filtering out the publications that match the exclusion criteria:

Final scrutiny of the papers was done based on the abstract and conclusion of the papers. A total of 134 studies were selected for this research. Among them, 61 papers were published in journals, 39 papers appeared in conference proceedings, 3 papers came from workshops, 2 papers were extracted from symposiums, 10 papers were from book chapters, and 9 papers were technical reports and 8 papers in others category. The respective percentages of the selected studies are represented in Figure 2 while the number of papers by year of publication is shown in Figure 3.

Table 1. Inclusion and exclusion criteria

Inclusion Criteria	Exclusion Criteria
All the papers published in the English language	Language is other than English
Papers that focus on risk assessment for improving requirements in particular	Studies whose findings are unclear and ambiguous
Paper having different types of proposals: Models, framework, techniques, tools, etc	Papers that are duplicate
Papers published from the year 1986	Paper focusing on risk assessment but not software engineering oriented.

Figure 2. Paper Distribution

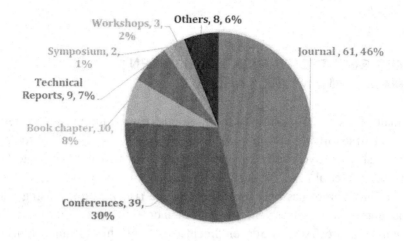

Figure 3. Number of papers by year of publication

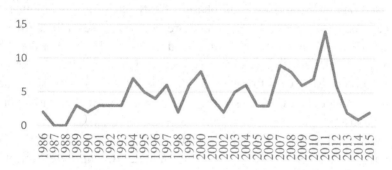

Research Questions

Following research questions are addressed in this study:

RQ1: What are the existing approaches used for risk assessment and management?

RQ2: What are the descriptions and limitations of existing risk assessment and management techniques?

RQ3: What are various dimensional scales of risk assessment factors each technique exhibit?

RQ4: What are different risk factors and perspectives adopted by stakeholders and developer for risk assessment and mitigation?

RQ5: What are various risk factors related to requirement schedule for risk assessment and management?

RQ6: Which risk management model fits the best for which phase of software lifecycle?

STUDIES RELATED TO RISK ASSESSMENT AND MANAGEMENT (RQ1 AND RQ2)

The demand for software solutions and high customer requirements creates stiff competition in the software development market. It would propel software companies to manage risks effectively and efficiently helping to improve the success-to-failure ratio (Wanderley et al., 2015). Analysis on the research in the last three decades shows that an attempt has been made to manage risk factors by using various methods, approaches, process and models for incrementing the success rate and decrementing failure in software development activities (Janjua, Jaafar & Lai, 2016). Risk assessment and management practices provide a structured and coherent way to assess and manage risk (Noraini & Bokolo, 2015). Various approaches in the past have focused on assessing risks in all phases of software life cycle, by integrating risk management practices at every juncture. However, several attempts have been made where risk assessment is integrated in the initial phase of the software development, which benefits the software project by handling risk at the early stage (Bhukya, Pabboju, 2018; Cornford et al., 2006). A set of studies have used structured and methodical models for risk assessment in which analytical hierarchy process, UML, decision trees, goal-oriented techniques, fuzzy entropy, risk metrics, machine learning and bayesian belief network were used (Hsieh, Hsu & Lin, 2016; Ghane, 2017; Meng, 2017; Zhi et al., 2017; Kamila & Sutikno, 2016; Cailliau & Lamsweerde, 2015; Anthony, 2015; Amber, Shawoo & Begum, 2012; Li & Liu, 2009; Kumar & Yadav, 2015). They culminate that the reduction in software risk is primarily due to effective risk management practices. Most of the risk management practices divide risk management into basic processes which start with identification of risk, further on to analysis, followed by mitigation and monitoring of risk (Guiling & Xiaojuan, 2011; Kumar, Sagar & Sudheer, 2010). Major studies perform risk analysis both qualitative and quantitatively which assesses risk based on probability and impact. Contrary, some models analyze risk related to software projects only. Some studies also work on project time delays which too is an indirect impact from software risk (Genuchten, 1991; Swede & Vliet, 1994). However, risk management is also dealt through research work in special cases like requirement engineering, risk-based QA and project risk dependencies (Amber, Shawoo & Begum, 2012; Lobato, Neto & Machado, 2012; Gallardo, 2012; Veenendaal, 2011). This section answers RQ1 and RQ2 and presents descriptions of existing risk assessment practices proposed till date in Table 2 followed by the limitations.

Table 2. Risk Assessment Methods

S. No	Method	Description
1	BOEHM (Boehm, 1991)	• It highlights the concept of "risk exposure" which is a relationship between the chances of occurrence of an unexpected event and the loss as a result. • Top ten risk identification checklist is identified and the decision tree method used to ascertain risk items. • The risk management approach has two steps, each subdivided into three steps. Risk assessment, the premier step involves risk identification, analysis, and prioritization. The second step is risk control which involves management planning, resolution, and monitoring of the risk. This model is applicable in all phases of software development.
2	SEI-SRE (Carr et al., 1993)	• SEI-SRE (Software Engineering Institute -Software Risk Evaluation) was developed by the Software Engineering Institute. This method is very efficient and is mainly used in defense IT projects. • Project manager expectations are managed by preparing high-level strategic plans for mitigating risk as a template. This paradigm shows a set of functions: identify, analyze, plan, track, control, and communicate. This is a continuous activity, which goes throughout the lifecycle of a project.
3	RISKIT (Kontio & Basili, 1997)	• This method defines risks more precisely and formally and provides support for multiple stakeholders by considering the definition of items which influence the project like goals, objectives, and drivers all of which are explicitly mentioned. • It models different aspects of risks qualitatively and prioritizes risk using ratio and ordinal scales. • This model is flexible and can be applied to many domains apart from of software development.
4	SERUM (Greer, 1997)	• Software Engineering Risk: Understanding and Management (SERUM) looks at both explicit and implicit risk making the risk management easier and handling them more adequately. • It is used in software released in versions and considers the risk in the current system as well as in proposed system. • Feedback of similar kind of projects does not account for in SERUM.
5	SERIM (Karolak, 1995)	• Software Engineering Risk Index Management model follows "Just in Time" strategy, it helps to assess risk factors from various analytical perspectives and develops action plans to risk management before they come live. • This method defines prior and urgent risk areas, develops proactive plans for risk mitigation • Ten risk factors are identified which are assessed quantitatively, by the project manager as lower the score the riskier projects.
6	SRAM (Foo & Muruganantham, 2000)	• This model considers the nine risk elements that are the complexity of software, project staff, targeted reliability, product requirement, a method of estimation, Monitoring practice, the process of development, usability of software/tools. • This model is questionnaire based and provides a quantitative assessment of risk with good accuracy.

continues on following page

Table 2. Continued

S. No	Method	Description
7	PRORISK (Suebkuna & Ramingwong, 2011)	• Project Oriented Risk Management Model is a decision support tool that works on linking project management and risk management in a software project. • It is a practical approach, which can be easily understood and efficiently applied in any software projects. Three important elements are risk management, project management, and risk database which is used to manage risk control information.
8	SRAEM (Gupta & Sadiq, 2008)	• In SRAEM (Software risk assessment and estimation model) estimation of risk is done using software metric and risk exposure based on Mission Critical Requirements Stability Risk Metrics (MCRSRM) • This model shows cumulative and phase-wise risk and handles the issues related to requirement analysis.
9	SRAEP (Sadiq et al., 2010)	• SRAEP (Software Risk Assessment and Evaluation Process) is a model-based approach which uses Software Fault Tree (SFT) for identifying a risk • Issues at the requirements phase are handled in this model.
10	SPRMQ (Mofleh & Zahary, 2011)	• SPRMQ (Software Product Risk Management based on Quality attributes and operational lifecycle) manages software product risk. • It has four processes: Identification of risk factors using brainstorming technique; analyze risk probabilities using probability/impact approach; risk mitigation using avoidance, minimization, and contingency strategy; and risk monitoring.
11	Soft Risk (Keshlaf & Hashim, 2000)	• Keshlaf and Hashim developed a prototyping tool called Soft Risk for managing software risks. • This model focuses on risk documentation and concentrates on top risks, it saves developers time and effort by reducing software risks to a great extent.
12	Agle et al. (2003)	• Agle et al. proposes effective handling of risk and handling team structure by knowledge building and effective communication. • This approach can only be used in a multi-team environment.
13	Hoodat and Rashidi (2009)	• This paper presents relations between classified risk using risk tree structure. • Risk analysis and assessment is done by Probabilistic calculations and helps in the qualitative and quantitative estimation of risk.
14	RIMAM (Shahzad & Al-Mudimigh, 2010)	• Risk Identification, Mitigation and Avoidance Model (RIMAM) highlight the strategies for risk identification, management, and avoidance of risk factors. • This model is used to check various risk factors due to an immature requirement, delivery deadline, etc. It is easily implemented with minimum cost and can be customized w.r.t the environment
15	TRM (Higuera et al., 1994)	• Team Risk Management focuses on customer-supplier risk management activities. • TRM establishes a set of processes including methods and tools that enable a relationship between the customer and supplier to work seamlessly.

continues on following page

Table 2. Continued

S. No	Method	Description
16	ARMOR (Lu et al., 1995)	• Analyzer for Reducing Module Operational Risk (ARMOR) is a tool for software risk analysis. It identifies the operational risks of all the software program modules. • It can measure software programs risks, identify the origin of risks and evaluate how to reduce their risk levels
17	RAT (Sharif & Rozan, 2010)	• RAT (Risk Analysis Tool) is used to do a hybrid assessment of risks • It is an expert system where the project manager can assess, monitors, and gives preliminary solutions automatically based on the project plan.
18	ERM (Snekir & Walker, 2007)	• Enterprise Risk Management (ERM) helps in identifying and minimize the risk that could cause an organization to fail to meet its strategies and objectives. • It includes risk associated with accidental losses and also financial, strategic, operational, and other risks
19	RMM (Hillson, 1997)	• RMM (Risk Maturity Model) provides the benchmark for an organization to check its maturity of handling risks in projects • Naïve, Novice, Normalized, and Natural are the four levels of maturity which are mapped to attributes culture, process, experience and application
20	Amber et al. (2012)	• A model is proposed for modeling and reasoning the risk at the requirements analysis phase and is based on UML oriented approach • The use case scenarios are handled using McCabe's cyclomatic complexity process. It helps in finding high-risk functional requirements.
21	Pandey et.al (2011)	• A framework is proposed that incorporate security requirement and risk management technique. It helps in improving the iterative security engineering activity at the initial phase of software development
22	Van Veenendaal (2011)	• PRISMA (Product Risk Management) is an approach for highlighting the parts having the maximum business and technical risk and support risk-based testing. • This approach can be used at each level of testing, and valid across organization and project level. It improves the effectiveness and efficiency of the defect detection process and is easy to use.
23	Nancy R. Mead (2012)	• Helps in determining security requirements engineering process using Security Quality Requirements Engineering (SQUARE) method • The SQUARE method has nine steps to categorizes and prioritizes security requirements • It can be used for any large-scale design project.
24	GSRM (Islam & Houmb, 2010)	• Islam and Houmb proposed a goal-driven software development risk management model (GSRM). Technical as well as non-technical development components are taken into consideration. • It effectively identifies and showcases the project goals, risk factors and control actions for mitigating risks and is advantageous at the initial phases of the development.

continues on following page

Table 2. Continued

S. No	Method	Description
25	Kwan and Leung (2011)	• This work handles risk dependency issues by introducing a management methodology • It details two sets of risk response strategies for posterior risks and other for risk dependencies. The communication between projects can be improved with this approach.
26	Nolan et al.(2011)	• This paper shows the use of requirement uncertainty analysis technique. This technique was used for Rolls-Royce traditional software development and explains how it operates regarding a software product line • The analysis technique reduces Scrap & Rework on a traditional project from an average of 50% to below 5%.
27	Lobato et al.(2012)	• The purpose is to identify SPL (Software Product Lines) risks while project scoping and requirement disciplines are in progress for a better understanding of risk management. • Benefits of applying SPL are generally related to business objectives and various organizational issues.
28	IRMAS (Khoo et al., 2007)	• This effort shows a quick risk mapping and assessment system (IRMAS) to support risk management for multi-site projects. The system follows the standard risk management framework (AS/NZS 4360, 1999). • It is extended to support risk tracking, reporting and risk management in other applications also.
29	RISICARE (Costa et al., 2007)	• RISICARE tool was planned and implemented to calculate project risk • Five modules are: Project characteristics, questionnaire, project portfolio, risk level, and simulation
30	Ropponen (2000)	• This paper presents a survey covering more than 80 project managers (1,100 projects), it shows how detailed know-how of environmental context and current managerial practices can be integrated with risk management considerations for managing software risks in an optimum manner.
31	Dey and Ogunlana (2007)	• A risk management framework is proposed from a developer perspective for software development projects and is user-friendly and simple • It uses a qualitative/quantitative technique with the stakeholder's involvement in the identification, analysis, and response to risk

RESULTS AND DISCUSSION

This section presents and discusses the findings of this study. The detailed description of the finding is presented by answering selected research questions.

Limitations of Existing Approaches (RQ2)

Many existing approaches have various limitations that are generally not addressed by practitioners. Here some of the main limitations of existing approaches are highlighted.

Many approaches address a limited number of goals, such as schedule and cost. There can be other important goals that can affect the success of the project and should be taken care of such as compatibility with other domain/systems, the reputation of the company, etc. Very few approaches support communication among stakeholders. It is known that risk perceptions can be influenced by various external factors, as the subjective element cannot be eliminated from the analysis of risk. Hence, it is essential to include a decision-making element in the risk assessment, to ensure its effectiveness it is essential to involve stakeholders in the decision-making.

Most risk frameworks only consider risk, which has a negative impact on the system. However, there are risks, which can have a positive impact on the system as opportunities, which are generally ignored by these approaches. Hence, it is required to cater to negative risk while enhancing the opportunities. The traditional risk-assessment techniques do not necessarily provide an easy guide of all potential risk to consider at a component/environment level. That is why systematic literature review is required on risk assessment tailored to the situations faced.

Dimensional Scales of Risk Assessment Techniques (RQ3)

Seven major dimensional scales of risk assessment practices have been identified as shown in Figure 4.

Williams et al. (1999), Foo and Murganantham (2000), Mc- Connell (1996) and Carr et al. (1993) proposed questionnaire-based risk assessment methods. Mc- Connell (1996) approach also covered coding issues and a list of schedule risk factors in their approach. Carr et al. (1993) introduced SEI risk taxonomy having three major groups: development environment, program constraints, and product engineering. This taxonomy has a hierarchical structure with 194 open questions from the software development risk perspective. Konito (2001) monitored brainstorming sessions and considered them useful for risk identification. Brainstorming session requires interaction among several project stakeholders to identify the risk in the project, it involves extensive human involvement. This technique has certain advantages

Figure 4. Risk assessment dimensional scales

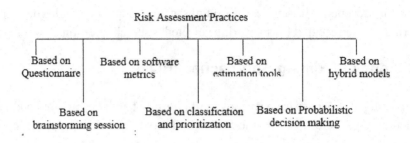

like improving the interaction, getting the response and concerned actions fast, etc. However, there are few limitations like non-availability of stakeholders when required, dependency on participant's expertise. Hyatt and Rosenberg (1996) used software metrics for risk assessment in the project where specific quality attributes and goals were defined. As an output metrics were defined which relates to software development practices. Gupta and Sadiq (2008) also used software metrics which identifies set of risk from each phase of software development and finds total cumulative risk. Sadiq et al. (2010) used SRAEP (Software Risk Assessment and Evaluation Process) which is based on fault tree method. Boehm (1991) used quantitative/qualitative assessment of risk in software projects. This model uses a decision tree for risk event classification based on their dependence. Uzzafer (2011) proposed a risk assessment model for generating cost estimates when integrated with models for cost estimation. This model focuses on the classification of risk events of software projects qualitatively. Fairley (1994) used attributes where congenial risk events like size, time, etc. to recognize the statistical dependence of the risk events. Keshlaf and Hashim (2000) worked on a generic tool for software risk management named SoftRisk. This model focuses on technical, cost, and schedule risks and is based on SERIM (Software Engineering risk model). However, they fail to deal with issues of requirement complexity. Sadiq et al. (2010) introduced a tool esrc Tool based on SRAEM model. It uses the function point approach and helps in estimating the risk and cost of the software.

Probabilistic decision-making techniques like Artificial Neural Networks (ANN) are also used to identify risk in software development. It is a machine learning technique which is helpful in solving problems which has unclear definition and not understood. Kutlubayet al. (2006) introduced a method using machine-learning methods for identifying software defects. Salvatore et al. (2007) did substantial work by improving the existing risk management models through equating the historical risk data of similar projects risks that were found with every framework through direct integration with stakeholders. Another study by Goonawardeneet al. (2010) where the use of neural and fuzzy systems is examined over various disparate areas like forecasting of project success, the decision on year-end appraisal or flavor on job recruiting. Fenton and Neil (1999) have proposed a model using Bayesian Belief Networks and shown that models using Bayesian Belief Networks are advantageous over the classical approaches. Fuzzy logic technique from many other forms is used to assess risks in new software projects. Li et al. (2009), proposed a model for expert assessment based on the fuzzy linguistic multiple attribute decision making. In this model risk assessment is done by prioritizing the risk based on a set of linguistic terms and on criteria which have been predefined for risk assessment. An approach using Fuzzy Inference system (Iranmanesh et al., 2009) uses Schmidt risk factors. Ekananta et al. (2013), introduced a Fuzzy expert-COCOMO model which integrates risk assessment with effort estimation. There are several researches where combinations of approaches are used like Deursen, and Kuipers (2003) introduced a method that has questionnaires integrated with software metrics. Hu et al. (2007) proposed a model using techniques like support vector machine (SVM), Neural Network (NN), and genetic algorithm approaches which are used for project risk assessment. The model is tested on data from questions answered, and SVM is seen to be better than NN. Then NN model is improved with a genetic algorithm to show better results.

Risk Factors and Perspectives Adopted by Developer and Stakeholders for Risk Assessment and Mitigation (RQ4)

Software Engineering Institute (SEI) (Stern & Arias, 2011; Carr et al., 1993; Tianyin, 2011) lists following risk factors listed in Table 3, which are associated with every software development because software development project holds unique and surprising elements of uncertainty.

In addition to the above factors, some commonly encountered factors are in direct control of project managers and have a substantial impact on the success of the project. This chapter provides a broad classification and discussion of these factors as discussed by various researchers in their work, as stakeholder perspective risk which is presented and discussed in Table 4.

Risk Factors Related to Requirement Schedule (RQ5)

In continuation of the discussion above there are risk factors related to requirement schedule, which have a severe impact. Table 5 presents and discusses all these factors.

Table 3. Potential SEI Risk factors (Developers perspective)

1	**Incorrect Resources estimation:** In case resourcing is not done correctly, the correct skills do not exist for finishing the work, the work items are assigned but do not get completed, it can get the managers jittery and completing the project shall be risky.
2	**User/Customer uncertainty:** The stakeholder consensus and presence is required for fetching details on the project work, the requirements are fetched, understanding validated, application output validated through users and customers without which objective cannot be met.
3	**Ambiguous requirements:** Unclear requirements, which either mean something else or are wrong, can cause loss of functionality to the application. The development team is not implementing against the correct objective and risky for delivery.
4	**Improper design risk:** If a design decision that is hard to change later gets put in the project, it shall be risky on delivery the product. The improper design can happen due to any reason associated with the project.
5	**Development system and risk with development system:** The tools used for development if not available or wrongly assigned can work towards the development team not starting to fulfill the correct objective, the risk is enormous on the completion.
6	**Inadequate management process:** The top management or project managers must support the execution of the project, disinterest in proceedings, manual processes, etc. can be significant risks due to which project completion can be an issue.
7	**Improper work environment:** The corporate culture or environments the team uses to implement should be proper and mimic environments which users want to visualize, an improper environment can cause a risk.

Table 4. Stakeholder Perspective Risk

S. No	Stakeholder Risk Perspective	Description
1	Lack of top management support	• Keil et al. (1998) found that if senior management lacks the commitment, it can end up being a disruptive risk • The top management attention and support is required throughout the project implementation. The management team has to prioritize the responsibilities and identify software projects as a top priority (Leitheiser, 1986; Barki & Hartwick, 1989; Gioia, 1996; Nah et al., 2001).
2	Corporate culture not supportive	• Corporate culture should be correctly placed, any unknown agenda can hamper delivery progress when ideas change based on will and not policy • This results in collaterally damaging the management support, as the objectives are not met (Baccarini et al., 2004; Leitheiser, 1986; Engming &Hsieh, 1994; Irani & Love, 2001).
3	Inadequate user involvement	• As per many researchers, it is one of the top ten causes of software failure • Client involvement and management is required in managing scope and objective, lack of which causes issues in budget and schedule (Keil et al.,1998; Zhou et al., 2008; Addison & Vallabh, 2002; Smith et al., 2006)
4	Lack of client responsibility and ownership	• Keil et al. (1998) identified this as a fundamental risk • User or client involvement in the software project helps in making a better product. When things go wrong, and the users are not involved, the project managers of the software project are generally blamed for the lack of client responsibility (Mursu et al., 1999).
5	Friction between clients and contractors	• Opposing ideas between vendors and software contractors cause operational problems and can have an adverse effect on the work which is another reason for the cause of friction (Jones, 1993).

Table 5. Requirement and Schedule Risk

S. No	Requirement and Schedule Risk	Description
1	Miscommunication of requirements	• Missing clarity or miscommunication is one of the causes due to which requirements are not understood correctly. It causes an original set of requirements and other information being wrong or wrongly understood (Iacovou & Nakatsu, 2008)
2	Unclear scope/objectives	• Different stakeholders have different objectives as explained by Boehm (1989) • These differences drive a clash in the understanding of the scope resulting in unclear and hazy requirements understanding. Ambiguous requirement specifications are more likely to create problems related to project budget and schedule (Boehm, 1989; Shull, 2000)
3	Changing requirements	• The stakeholders often modify the requirements based on business values and user's need. However, frozen requirements do enable the completion of the project on time, but they would not be able to accommodate changes. • It has been shown that continuous changes in the requirements enviably lead to affect the schedule (Keil, 1998; Mursu et al., 2009; Jones,1993; King, 1994)
4	Improper change management	• Improper change management often hurts the stability of the application and increases cost in operations/support, which becomes a significant cause for software failure (Smith, 2006; Rasmussen et al., 2006; Han & Huang, 2007; Keil et al., 2002).
5	Unrealistic schedule and budget	• Sometimes the planning for the project is not done diligently, and the project does not reach completion due to either a very rigorous schedule or lower budget. • A fixed schedule might lead to work completion pressures which can have risk on the timely schedule or project results output (Boehm, 1989; King, 1994; Turner, 1999; Hamid et al., 1999).
6	Misunderstanding of requirements	• If the requirement is not understood clearly, it can take multiple cycles of clarification from stakeholders resulting in a delay of the software project. It is one of the significant risks in software projects which affects the project (Keil, 1998; Field, 1997; Schmidt et al., 2001; Addison & Vallabh, 2002; Mursu et al., 2009).
7	Unrealistic expectations	• Keil et al. (1998) pointed out that if the user expectations are incorrect or unrealistic, the project cannot be planned and completed. • Sometimes, internally wrong expectations are set through top management that causes even further issues in the team.
8	Gold plating	• The developers can add features to make system attractive and application sustainable but sometimes increases the cost and make users unhappy (Boehm, 1989; Cunningham, 1999).
9	Inaccurate estimation of schedule or cost	• A wrong estimate can be detrimental for the project. If the estimate were wrong, it would follow with the wrong budget and resulting delay in release. Both under-estimating and overestimating leads to multiple issues with the projects (Galorath, 2006; Masticola, 2007).

Mapping of Various Risk Assessment and Management Models with Software Lifecycle Phases (RQ6)

It can be observed that risk(s) in software projects can happen in any of phase of SDLC. Therefore, it is essential to map models/strategies with different phases of SLDC, in order to analyze which risk management model fits the best for which phase of the software lifecycle. Table 6 outlines this mapping.

Table 6. Risk models mapping with phases of SDLC (Roy, Dasgupta & Chaki, 2016)

S. No	Methods/ Models	Purpose	Risk considered	SDLC Phases
1	BOEHM (1991)	Risk Identification, analysis, Prioritization, control	Generic risks (a risk that is a potential threat to every software project) and project-specific risks	Requirement analysis and planning
2	SoftRisk (Keshlaf & Hashim, 2000)	Risk identification, assessment, monitoring		Requirement and planning phase, maintenance phase
3	ARMOR (Lu et al., 1995)	Risk Identification, analysis	All program module risks	
4	PRORISK (Suebkuna & Ramingwong, 2011)	Risk assessment, risk control	Software related Generic risks	Requirement phase, coding phase, maintenance phase
5	RMM (Hillson, 1997)	Risk assessment	Organizational risks	Not followed
6	ERM (Snekir & Walker, 2007)	Risk identification, assessment	Generic risks and project-specific risks	
7	RAT (Sharif & Rozan, 2010)	Risk assessment, treatment and monitoring	Projects risks of Small and medium software	
8	TRM (Higuera et al., 1994)	Risk analysis, mitigation	Team risks	
9	Agle et al. (2003)	Risk handling	Risk related to team structure	
10	SEI-SRE (Carr et al., 1993)	Risk Evaluation: Detection, specification, assessment, consolidation, mitigation	Product risks, Process risks	Requirement phase, coding phase, testing phase, maintenance phase
11	SRAM (Foo & Muruganantham, 2000)	Risk assessment, prioritization	Development risk	Requirement analysis
12	Armestrong (2008)	Risk identification	Economic risk, business risk	
13	RISKIT (Kontio & Basili, 1997)	Risk identification, analysis, monitoring, prioritize as per probability and impact	Generic risk, project risk, technical risk, schedule risk, business risk	Requirement phase, application, and maintenance phase
14	Hoodat and Rashidi (2009)	Risk measurement	Project risk, product risk, schedule risk, cost risk, quality risk, business risk	Planning phase, testing and debugging phase, application phase.

continues on following page

Table 6. Continued

S. No	Methods/ Models	Purpose	Risk considered	SDLC Phases
15	SERIM (Karolak, 1995)	Risk assessment, risk ranking	Technical risk, cost risk, schedule risk, organizational risk, application risk	Requirement analysis and planning phase
16	RIMAM (Shahzad & Al-Mudimigh, 2010)	Risk identification, management, avoidance	schedule risk and cost risk	
17	SRAEM (Gupta & Sadiq, 2008)	Risk estimation	technical risk, organization risk, environmental risk	
18	SRAEP (Sadiq et al., 2010)	Risk assessment, prioritization		
19	SERUM (Greer, 1997)	Implicit and explicit risk management	Generic risk, risk related to planning, development risk	
20	SPRMQ (Mofleh & Zahary, 2011)	risk factor identification, risk probability computation, effects on product quality, risk mitigation and monitoring	Product risks	
21	Danny (2013)	Risk mitigation	Operational risk	Application phase

SUMMARY OF CURRENT STATE OF ART

This section summarizes the current state of the art in practice for risk management:

- A few frameworks are available which follow similar kind of process to manage the risks in the software projects. Many researchers have emphasized to initiate risk management early in the software project lifecycle but how to integrate still has credible questions. Some work considering risk management has been done in software design (Verdon & McGraw, 2004) though on analysis a change of design or re-elicitation of requirements can have an adverse effect on the project and other work is done in requirement engineering (Borland, 2005; Boness et al., 2008). The real risk management tasks happen at the forefront of the project helping to curtail problems.
- The most prevalent practice in software risk management has significant impetus on schedule and budget. Nowadays, new goals have gained importance such as stakeholder consensus, market delighter, integration, etc. The new goals need to be focused on for viewing the risks in requirements from a holistic software development perspective.
- Risk Management in the software industry is still naive; many frameworks have been developed for performing software risk management activities (Karolak, 1995; Boehm, 1991; Karolak, 1995; Kontio, 2001). The implementation of the risk management activities is still not applied and practiced (Ropponen,

1999; Pfleeger, 2000) The project managers know about the risks and its effects but the effort concentrates on minimizing the cost and time in the project, and that is why risk management does not hold a high priority.

- Several taxonomies are available for categorizing requirement defects, they help in effectively managing defect detection and prevention (Alshazly et al., 2014; Beizer, 1990; Chillarege et al., 1992; Grady, 1992; Margarido, Faria, Vidal & Vieira, 2011; Walia & Carver, 2009; Hayes, 2003). In the past, there have been few methods and defect taxonomies used on validation of requirements (Ackerman, Buchwald & Lewski,1989; Sommerville, 2004; Laitenberger, Atkinson, Schlich & Emam, 2000; Felderer & Beer, 2013, 2015). However, they are used in the later part of the software lifecycle and not really on requirement validation (Felderer & Beer, 2013, 2015) and only little has been done in that direction. Hence, there is a need to focus and put more onus on relating requirements to defect taxonomy to find the risk in them.

- The traditional/old risk management practice is followed by a majority of project managers that tends to concentrate really on the potential negative risk or issues by spending considerable effort on identifying and managing threats, ignoring the positive side of risk (Hillson, 2002). More focus is needed on enhancing and exploring the opportunities in the project as well.

CONCLUSION

The primary objective of this study was to present a systematic literature review of techniques/methods/tools for risk assessment and management. This research identifies and discovers existing risk assessment and management techniques, their limitations, taxonomies, and processes. The goal of this study was to discover potential problems and identify possible improvements for better defect identification and prevention. It can be concluded that there is a need to focus on the effect of executing every single requirement from the viewpoint of risk it can pose to the system under development. It is essential to identify and analyze various requirement defects before a decision of inclusion of a requirement is taken. These defect prevention techniques or models are necessary and essential in order to be sure that all business requirements are captured correctly (with clear vision and scope), and only the correct requirements which focus on delivering value to the customer are selected by taking a right decision using risk estimation. This research will help the research community to improve software quality by developing more effective tools and methods.

REFERENCES

Ackerman, A. F., Buchwald, L. S., & Lewski, F. H. (1989). Software Inspections: An Effective Verification Process. *IEEE Software*, *6*(3), 31–36. doi:10.1109/52.28121

Addison, T., & Vallabh, S. (2002). Controlling software project risks: An empirical study of methods used by experienced project managers. In *Proceedings of SAICSIT*. Port Elizabeth, South Africa: ACM.

Alge, B. J., Witheoff, C., & Klein, H. J. (2003). When does the Medium matter? Knowledge building experiences and opportunities in decision-making teams. *Organizational Behavior and Human Decision Processes*, *91*(1), 26–37. doi:10.1016/S0749-5978(02)00524-1

Alshazly, A. A., Elfatatry, A. M., & Abougabal, M. S. (2014). Detecting defects in software requirements specification. *Alexandria Engineering Journal*, *53*(3), 513–527. doi:10.1016/j.aej.2014.06.001

Amber, S., Shawoo, N., & Begum, S. (2012). Determination of Risk During Requirement Engineering Process. *International Journal of Emerging Trends in Computing and Information Sciences*, *3*(3), 358–364.

Anthony, B., Noraini, C. P., Nor, R. N. H., & Jusoh, Y. Y. (2015). A risk assessment model for collaborative support in software management. *9th Malaysian Software Engineering Conference (MySEC)*, 217-223. 10.1109/MySEC.2015.7475224

Armestrong, R., & Adens, G. (2008). Managing Software Project Risks. TASSC Technical Paper.

Arshad, N. R., Mohamed, A., & Matnor, Z. (2007). Risk factors in software development projects. In *Proceedings of the 6th WSEAS international conference on software engineering, parallel and distributed systems*. Corfu Island, Greece: ACM.

Avdoshin, S. M., & Pesotskaya, E. Y. (2011). Software risk management. *Proceedings of 7th Central and Eastern European Software Engineering Conference*, 1-6.

Baccarini, D., Salm, G., & Love, P. E. D. (2004). Management of risks in information technology projects. *Industrial Management & Data Systems*, *10*(4), 286–295. doi:10.1108/02635570410530702

Barki, H., & Hartwick, J. (1989). Rethinking the concept of user involvement. *Management Information Systems Quarterly*, *13*(1), 53–63. doi:10.2307/248700

Beizer, B. (1990). *Software testing techniques (2nded.)*. New York, NY: Van Nostrand Reinhold.

Bhukya, S. N., & Pabboju, S. (2018). Software engineering: Risk features in requirement engineering. *Cluster Computing*, 1–13.

Boehm, B. (1981). *Software Engineering Economics*. Prentice- Hall.

Boehm, B. W. (1989). Organizational Climate and Culture. Jossey-Bass.

Boehm, B. W. (1991). Software Risk Management: Principles and Practices. *IEEE Software*, 8(1), 32–41. doi:10.1109/52.62930

Boness, K., Finkelstein, A., & Harrison, R. (2008). A lightweight technique for assessing risks in requirements analysis. *IET Software*, 2(1), 46–57. doi:10.1049/iet-sen:20070068

Borland. (2005). *Mitigating risk with effective requirements engineering*. Technical report, White paper.

Cailliau, A., & Lamsweerde, A. (2015). Handling knowledge uncertainty in risk-based requirements engineering. *IEEE 23rd International Requirements Engineering Conference (RE)*, 106-115.

Carr, M., Konda, S., Monarch, I., Ulrich, C., & Walker, C. (1993). *Taxonomy based risk identification. Technical report*. Pittsburgh, PA: Software Engineering Institute, Carnegie Mellon University. doi:10.21236/ADA266992

Chillarege, R., Bhandari, I. S., Chaar, J. K., Halliday, M. J., Moebus, D. S., Ray, B. K., & Wong, M. Y. (1992). Orthogonal Defect Classification-A Concept for In-Process Measurements. *IEEE Transactions on Software Engineering*, 18(11), 943–956. doi:10.1109/32.177364

Cornford, S. L., Feather, M. S., Heron, V. A., & Jenkins, J. S. (2006). Fusing quantitative requirements analysis with model-based systems engineering. *Proceedings of the 14th IEEE international requirements engineering conference*, 279–284. 10.1109/RE.2006.24

Costa, H. R., Barros, M. D. O., & Travassos, G. H. (2007). Evaluating software project portfolio risks. *Journal of Systems and Software*, 80(1), 16–31. doi:10.1016/j.jss.2006.03.038

Cunningham, M. (1999). It's all about the business. *Inform (Silver Spring, Md.)*, 13(3), 83.

Danny, L. (2013). Reducing Operational Risk by improving production software quality. *Software Risk Reduction Rev, 13*, 1–15.

Deursen, T., & Kuipers, A. V. (2003). Source-Based Software Risk Assessment. In *Proceedings of the International Conference on Software Maintenance*. Los Alamitos, CA: IEEE Computer Society.

Dey, P. K., Kinch, J., & Ogunlana, S. O. (2007). Managing risk in software development projects: A case study. *Industrial Management & Data Systems*, *107*(2), 284–303. doi:10.1108/02635570710723859

Ekananta, M., Capretz, L. F., & Ho, D. (2013). Software Project Risk Assessment and Effort Contingency Model based on COCOMO Cost Factors. *Journal of Computations and Modeling*, *3*(1), 113–132.

Engming, L., & Hsieh, C. T. (1994). Seven deadly risk factors of software development projects. *Journal of Systems Management*, *36*(6), 38–42.

Fairley, R. (1994). Risk Management for Software Projects. *IEEE Software*, *11*(3), 57–67. doi:10.1109/52.281716

Felderer, M., & Beer, A. (2013). Using Defect Taxonomies for Requirements Validation in Industrial Projects. In *Proceedings of the 21st IEEE International Requirements Engineering Conference(RE)*. Rio de Janeiro, Brasil: IEEE. 10.1109/RE.2013.6636733

Felderer, M., & Beer, A. (2015). Using Defect Taxonomies for Testing Requirements. *IEEE Software*, *32*(3), 94–101. doi:10.1109/MS.2014.56

Fenton, N., & Neil, M. (1999). A Critique of Software Defect Prediction Models. *IEEE Transactions on Software Engineering*, *25*(5), 675–689. doi:10.1109/32.815326

Field, T. (1997). When BAD things Happen to GOOD projects. *CIO (Framingham, Mass.)*, 55–62.

Foo, S. W., & Muruganantham, A. (2000). Software risk assessment model. *Proceedings of the 2000 IEEE International Conference on Management of Innovation and Technology*, *2*, 536-544.

Gallardo, E. (2012). Using Configuration Management and Product Line Software Paradigms to Support the Experimentation Process in Software Engineering. *Proceedings of International Conference on Research Challenges in Information Science RCIS-2012*, 1-6. 10.1109/RCIS.2012.6240454

Galorath, D. D., & Evans, M. W. (2006). *Software Sizing Estimation and Risk Management*. Auerbach Publications. doi:10.1201/9781420013122.ch10

Genuchten, M. V. (1991). Why is software late? An empirical study of reasons for delay in software development. *IEEE Transactions on Software Engineering, 17*(6), 582–590. doi:10.1109/32.87283

Ghane, K. (2017). *Quantitative planning and risk management of Agile Software Development. In IEEE Technology & Engineering Management Conference* (pp. 109–112). Santa Clara, CA: TEMSCON.

Gioia, J. (1996). Twelve Reasons Why Programs Fail. *PM Network, 10*(11), 16–19.

Glass, R. L. (1998). *Software Runaways: Monumental Software Disasters*. Upper Saddle River, NJ: Prentice-Hall, Inc.

Goonawardene, N., Subashini, S., Boralessa, N., & Premaratne, L. (2010). A Neural Network Based Model for Project Risk and Talent Management. In *International Symposium on Neural Networks* (vol. 6064, pp. 532-539). Springer. 10.1007/978-3-642-13318-3_66

Grady, R. B. (1992). *Practical Software Metrics for Project Management and Process Improvement*. Upper Saddle River, NJ: Prentice-Hall.

Greer, D. (1997). SERUM - Software Engineering Risk: Understanding and Management. *Journal of Project and Business Risk Management, 1*(4), 373–388.

Guiling, L., & Xiaojuan, Z. (2011). Research on the risk management of IT project. *Proceedings of International conf. on E-Business and E -Government (ICEE),* 1-4.

Gupta, D., & Sadiq, M. (2008). Software Risk Assessment and Estimation Model. In *International Conference on Computer Science and International Technology*. IEEE Computer Society.

Hall, T., Beecham, S., & Rainer, A. (2002). Requirements problems in twelve software companies: An empirical analysis. *IEEE Software, 149*(5), 153–160. doi:10.1049/ip-sen:20020694

Hamid, A., Sengupta, T. K., & Swett, C. (1999). The Impact of Goals on Software Project Management: An Experimental Investigation. *Management Information Systems Quarterly, 23*(4), 531–555. doi:10.2307/249488

Han, W. M., & Huang, S. J. (2007). An empirical analysis of risk components and performance on software projects. *Journal of Systems and Software, 80*(1), 42–50. doi:10.1016/j.jss.2006.04.030

Hayes, J. H. (2003). Building a Requirement Fault Taxonomy: Experiences from a NASA Verification and Validation Research Project. In *Proceedings of the 14thInternational Symposium on Software Reliability Engineering (ISSRE'03)*. Denver, CO: IEEE Computer Society.

Higuera, R. P., Gluch, D. P., Dorofee, A. J., & Murphy, R. L. (1994). An introduction to team risk management. Software Engineering Institute. CMU/SEI-94-SR-001.

Hillson, D. A. (1997). Towards Risk Maturity Model. *International Journal of Project and Business Risk Management*, *1*(1), 35–45.

Hillson, D. A. (2002). Extending the risk process to manage opportunities. *International Journal of Project Management*, *20*(3), 235–240. doi:10.1016/S0263-7863(01)00074-6

Hoodat, H., & Rashidi, H. (2009). Classification and Analysis of Risks in Software Engineering. *World Academy of Science. Engineering and Technology WASET*, *3*(8), 446–452.

Hsieh, M. Y., Hsu, Y. C., & Lin, C. T. (2016). Risk assessment in new software development projects at the front end: A fuzzy logic approach. *Journal of Ambient Intelligence and Humanized Computing*. doi:0.100712652-016-0372-5

Hu, Y., Huang, J., Chen, J., Liu, M., & Xie, K. (2007). Software project risk management modelling with neural network and support vector machine approaches. In *Third International Conference on Natural Computation*. Washington, DC: IEEE Computer Society.

Hyatt, L., & Rosenberg, L. (1996). A Software Quality Model Metrics for Risk Assessment. *European Space Agency Software Assurance Symposium*.

Iacovou, C. L., & Nakatsu, R. (2008). A risk profile of offshore-outsourced development projects. *Communications of the ACM*, *51*(6), 89–94. doi:10.1145/1349026.1349044

IEEE. (1998). IEEE Standard for Software Reviews, IEEE Std 1028– 1997. IEEE.

Irani, Z., & Love, P. E. D. (2001). The propagation of technology management taxonomies for evaluating information systems. *Journal of Management Information Systems*, *17*(3), 161–177.

Iranmanesh, S. H., Khodadadi, B., & Taheri, S. (2009). Risk Assessment of Software Projects Using Fuzzy Inference System. *International Conference on Computers and Industrial Engineering*, 1149-1154. 10.1109/ICCIE.2009.5223859

Islam, S., & Houmb, S. H. (2010). Integrating Risk Management Activities into Requirements Engineering. *Fourth IEEE International Conference on Research Challenges in Information Science RCIS-2010*, 299-310. 10.1109/RCIS.2010.5507389

Janjua, U., Jaafar, J., & Lai, F. (2016). Expert's opinions on software project effective risk management. *Proceedings of 3rd International Conference on Computer and Information Sciences (ICCOINS)*, 471-476. 10.1109/ICCOINS.2016.7783261

Jones, C. (1993). *Assessment and Control of Software Risks*. Englewood Cliffs, NJ: Prentice-Hall.

Kamila, A. R., & Sutikno, S. (2016). Analysis of cause and effect relationship risk using fishbone diagram in SDLC SPASI v. 4.0 business process. In *International Conference on Information Technology Systems and Innovation (ICITSI)*. Bandung: IEEE.

Karolak, D. W. (1995). *Software Engineering Risk Management. IEEE Computer Society*. Los Alamitos, CA: Wiley.

Keil, M., Cule, P., Lyytinen, K., & Schmidt, R. (1998). A framework for identifying software project risks. *Communications of the ACM*, *41*(11), 76–83. doi:10.1145/287831.287843

Keil, M., Tiwana, A., & Bush, A. (2002). Reconciling user and project manager perceptions of IT project risk: A Delphi study. *Information Systems Journal*, *12*(2), 103–119. doi:10.1046/j.1365-2575.2002.00121.x

Keshlaf, A. A., & Hashim, K. (2000). A Model and Prototype Tool to Manage Software Risks. In *Proceedings of the 1st Asia-Pacific Conference on Quality Software (AP AQS'00)*. Washington, DC: IEEE.

Khoo, Y. B., Zhou, M., Kayis, B., Savci, S., Ahmed, A., Kusumo, R., & Rispler, A. (2007). IRMAS-development of a risk management tool for collaborative multi-site, multi-partner new product development projects. *Journal of Manufacturing Technology Management*, *18*(4), 387–414. doi:10.1108/17410380710743770

King, J. (1994). Sketchy plans, politics stall software development. *Computerworld*, *29*(24), 81.

Kontio, J. (2001). *Software Engineering Risk Management: A Method, Improvement Framework and Empirical Evaluation* (Ph.D. thesis). Helsinki University of Technology.

Kontio, J., & Basili, V. R. (1997). Empirical Evaluation of a Risk Management Method. *SEI Conference on Risk Management*, Atlantic City, NJ.

Krasner, H. (1998). Looking over the legal edge of unsuccessful software projects. *Cutter IT Journal, 11*(3), 11–22.

Kumar, C., & Yadav, D. (2015). A Probabilistic Software Risk Assessment and Estimation Model for Software Projects. *Procedia Computer Science, 54,* 353–361. doi:10.1016/j.procs.2015.06.041

Kumar, N. S., Vinay, S. A., & Sudheer, Y. (2010). Software Risk Management- An Integrated Approach. *Global Journal of Computer Science and Technology, 10*(15), 53–57.

Kutlubay, O., Bener, A., & Ceylan, E. (2006). Software Defect Identification Using Machine Learning Techniques. *Proceedings of Conference on Software Engineering and Advanced Applications (EUROMICRO-SEAA 2006).*

Kwan, T. W., & Leung, H. K. N. (2011). A Risk Management Methodology for Project Risk Dependencies. *IEEE Transactions on Software Engineering, 37*(5), 635–648. doi:10.1109/TSE.2010.108

Laitenberger, O., Atkinson, C., Schlich, M., & El Emam, K. (2000). An experimental comparison of reading techniques for defect detection in UML design documents. *Journal of Systems and Software, 53*(2), 183–204. doi:10.1016/S0164-1212(00)00052-2

Leitheiser, R. L., & Wetherbe, J. C. (1986). Service Support Levels: An Organized Approach to End-User Computing. *Management Information Systems Quarterly, 10*(4), 336–350.

Li, X., & Liu, Q. (2009). Requirement Risk Assessment Focused-on Stakeholder Risk Analysis. *Proceedings of 33rd Annual IEEE International Computer Software and Applications Conference, COMPSAC '09, 1,* 640-641. 10.1109/COMPSAC.2009.199

Li, Y., & Li, N. (2009). Software project risk assessment based on fuzzy linguistic multiple attribute decision making. *IEEE International Conference on Grey Systems and Intelligent Services,* 1163-1166. 10.1109/GSIS.2009.5408087

Lindquist, C. (2005). Required: Fixing the requirements mess; The requirements process, literally, deciding what should be included in the software, is destroying projects in ways that aren't evident until its too late. Some CIOs are stepping in to rewrite the rules. *CIO (Framingham, Mass.), 19*(4), 53–60.

Lobato, L. L. (2012). Risk Management in Software Product Lines: An Industrial Case Study. *Proceedings of International Conference on Software and System Process ICSSP,* 180-189. 10.1109/ICSSP.2012.6225963

Lobato, L. L., Neto, P. A., & Machado, I. (2012). A Study on Risk Management for Software Engineering. *Proceedings of 16th International Conference on Evaluation and Assessment in Software Engineering*, 47-51. 10.1049/ic.2012.0006

Lu, M. R., Yu, J. S., Keramidas, E., & Dalal, S. R. (1995). ARMOR: analyzer for reducing module operational risk. *Twenty-Fifth International Symposium on Fault-Tolerant Computing. Digest of Papers*, 137-142. 10.1109/FTCS.1995.466989

Margarido, I. L., Faria, J. P., Vidal, R. M., & Vieira, M. (2011). Classification of defect types in requirements specifications: Literature review, proposal, and assessment. Paper Presented at *6th Iberian Conference on Information Systems and Technologies (CISTI)*, Chaves, Portugal.

Masticola, S. P. (2007). A simple estimate of the cost of software project failures and the breakeven effectiveness of project risk management. In *Proceedings of the First International Workshop on the Economics of Software and Computation*. IEEE. 10.1109/ESC.2007.1

McConnell, S. (1996). *Rapid Development, Taming wild software schedules*. Microsoft Press.

McConnell, S. (1997). *Software Project Survival Guide: How to Be Sure Your First Important Project Isn't Your Last*. Redmond, WA: Microsoft Press.

Mead, N. R. (2012). Measuring The Software Security Requirements Engineering Process. *Proceedings of 36th International Conference on Computer Software and Application Workshops*, 583-588. 10.1109/COMPSACW.2012.107

Meng, Y. (2017). Study on software project risk assessment based on fuzzy analytic hierarchy process. *IEEE 3rd Information Technology and Mechatronics Engineering Conference (ITOEC)*, 853-857.

Mofleh, H. M., & Zahary, A. (2011). A Framework for Software Product Risk Management Based on Quality Attributes and Operational Life Cycle (SPRMQ). *12th International Arab Conference on Information Technology ACIT'2011*, Riyadh, Saudi Arabia.

Mursu, A., Soriyan, H. A., Korpela, M., & Olufokunbi, K. C. (1999). Toward Successful ISD in Developing Countries: First Results from a Nigerian Risk Study Using the Delphi Method. *Proceedings of the 22nd Information Systems Research Seminar in Scandinavia*.

Nah, F., Lau, J., & Kuang, J. (2001). Critical factors for successful implementation of enterprise systems. *Business Process Management Journal, 7*(3), 285–296. doi:10.1108/14637150110392782

Nolan, A. J., Abrahão, S., Clements, P. C., & Pickard, A. (2011). Requirements Uncertainty in a Software Product Line. In *Proceedings of 15th International Software Product Line Conference*. Munich, Germany: IEEE. 10.1109/SPLC.2011.13

Noraini, C. P., & Bokolo, A. J. (2015). A Review on Decision Making of Risk Mitigation for Software Management. *Journal of Theoretical and Applied Information Technology, 76*, 333–341.

Pandey, D., Suman, U., & Ramani, A. K. (2011). Security Requirement Engineering Issues in Risk Management. *International Journal of Computers and Applications, 17*(5), 11–14. doi:10.5120/2218-2827

Pfleeger, S. L. (2000). Risky business: What we have yet to learn about risk management. *Journal of Systems and Software, 53*(3), 265–273. doi:10.1016/S0164-1212(00)00017-0

Pohl, K., & Rupp, C. (2010). *Basiswissen Requirements Engineering* (2nd ed.). Heidelberg, Germany: Dpunkt Verlag. doi:10.1007/978-3-642-12578-2

Project Management Institute. (2017). A guide to the project management body of knowledge (PMBOK ® guide) (6th ed.). Author.

Rabia, H., & Muhammad, A. (2013). Critical success factors assessment in Software Projects. *Science and Information Conference*, London, UK.

Rasmussen, M., Orlov, L. M., & Bright, S. (2006). *Taking Control Of IT Risk Defining A Comprehensive IT Risk Management Strategy*. Forrester Research.

Ropponen, J. (1999). Risk assessment and management practices in software development. In L. P. Willcocks & S. Lester (Eds.), *Beyond the IT Productivity Paradox* (pp. 247–266). Chichester, UK: John Wiley & Sons.

Ropponen, J., & Lyytinen, K. (2000). Component of Software Development Risk: How to address them? A project manager survey. *IEEE Transactions on Software Engineering, 26*(2), 98–112. doi:10.1109/32.841112

Roy, B., Dasgupta, R., & Chaki, N. (2016). A Study on Software Risk Management Strategies and Mapping with SDLC. In R. Chaki, A. Cortesi, K. Saeed, & N. Chaki (Eds.), *Advanced Computing and Systems for Security. Advances in Intelligent Systems and Computing, 396*. New Delhi: Springer. doi:10.1007/978-81-322-2653-6_9

Sadiq, M., Rahman, A., Ahmad, S., Asim, M., & Ahmad, J. (2010). esrcTool: A Tool to Estimate the Software Risk and Cost. *IEEE second International Conference on Computer Research and development*, 886-890.

Sadiq, M., Rahmani, M. K. I., Ahmad, M. W., & Jung, S. (2010). Software risk assessment and evaluation process (SRAEP) using model-based approach. In *International Conference on Networking and Information Technology (ICNIT)*. Manila: IEEE. 10.1109/ICNIT.2010.5508535

Sarci, S. A., Cantone, G., & Basili, V. R. (2007). A Statistical Neural Network Framework for Risk Management Process - From the Proposal to its Preliminary Validation for Efficiency. *Proceedings of the Second International Conference on Software and Data Technologies*.

Schmidt, R., Lyytinen, K., Keil, M., & Cule, P. (2001). Identifying software project risks: An international Delphi study. *Journal of Management Information Systems*, *17*(4), 5–36. doi:10.1080/07421222.2001.11045662

Shahzad, B., & Al-Mudimigh, A. S. (2010). Risk Identification, Mitigation and Avoidance Model for Handling Software Risk. In *Proceedings of the 2010 2nd International Conference on Computational Intelligence, Communication Systems and Networks*. Liverpool, UK: ACM.

Sharif, A. M., & Rozan, M. Z. A. (2010). Design and Implementation of Project Time Management Risk Assessment Tool for SME Projects using Oracle Application Express. *World Academy of Science, Engineering and Technology*, *65*, 1221–1226.

Shull, F., Rus, I., & Basili, V. (2000). How perspective-based reading can improve requirements inspections. *Computer*, *33*(7), 73–79. doi:10.1109/2.869376

Smith, D., Eastcroft, M., Mahmood, N., & Rode, H. (2006). Risk factors affecting software projects in South Africa. *South African Journal of Business Management*, *37*(2), 55–65.

Snekir, W. G., & Walker, P. L. (2007). Enterprise Risk Management: Tools and Techniques for effective implementation. Institute of Management Accounts, 1-31.

Sommerville, I. (2004). *Software Engineering* (7th ed.). Pearson Addison Wesley.

Stern, R., & Arias, J. C. (2011). Review of Risk Management Methods. *Business Intelligence Journal*, *4*(1), 59–78.

Suebkuna, B., & Ramingwong, S. (2011). Towards a complete project-oriented risk management model: A refinement of PRORISK. In *Eighth International Joint Conference on Computer Science and Software engineering (JCSSE)*. IEEE. 10.1109/JCSSE.2011.5930146

Swede, V. V., & Vliet, J. V. (1994). Consistent development: results of a first empirical study on the relation between project scenario and success. In G. Wijers, S. Brinkkemper, & T. Wasserman (Eds.), Lecture Notes in Computer Science: Vol. 811. *Advanced Information Systems Engineering, CAiSE 1994*. Berlin: Springer.

Tianyin, P. (2011). Development of software project risk management model review. *Proceedings of International conference on Artificial Intelligence, Management Science and Electronic Commerce*, 2979-2982. 10.1109/AIMSEC.2011.6011139

Turner, J. R. (1999). Project Management: A profession based on knowledge or faith. *International Journal of Project Management, 17*(6), 329–342.

Uzzafer, M. (2011). A Novel Risk Assessment Model for Software Projects. *International Conference on Computer and Management (CAMAN)*, 1-5. 10.1109/CAMAN.2011.5778729

Veenendaal, E. V. (2011). Practical Risk-Based Testing - Product Risk Management: The PRISMA Method. EuroSTAR-2011, 1-24.

Verdon, D., & McGraw, G. (2004). Risk analysis in software design. *IEEE Security and Privacy, 2*(4), 79–84. doi:10.1109/MSP.2004.55

Walia, G. S., & Carver, J. C. (2009). A systematic literature review to identify and classify software requirement errors. *Information and Software Technology, 51*(7), 1087–1109. doi:10.1016/j.infsof.2009.01.004

Wanderley, M. Jr, Menezes, J. Jr, Gusmão, C., & Lima, F. (2015). Proposal of Risk Management Metrics for Multiple Project Software Development. *Procedia Computer Science, 64*, 1001–1009. doi:10.1016/j.procs.2015.08.619

Williams, R. C., Pandelios, G. J., & Behrens, S. G. (1999). *Software Risk Evaluation (SRE) Method description (Version-2.0)*. Technical report CMU/SEI-99-TR-029.

Zhi, H., Zhang, G., Liu, Y., & Shen, Y. (2017). A novel risk assessment model on software system combining modified fuzzy entropy-weight and AHP. *IEEE 8th Conference on Software Engineering and Service Science*, 451-454.

Zhou, L., Vasconcelos, A., & Nunes, M. (2008). Supporting decision making in risk management through an evidence-based information systems project risk checklist. *Information Management & Computer Security*, *16*(2), 166–186. doi:10.1108/09685220810879636

ADDITIONAL READING

Bannerman, P. (2008). Risk and risk management in software projects: A reassessment. *Journal of Systems and Software*, *81*(12), 2118–2133. doi:10.1016/j.jss.2008.03.059

Boehm, B., & Basili, V. (2001). Software Defect Reduction Top 10 List. *IEEE Computer*, *34*(1), 135–137. doi:10.1109/2.962984

CHAOS Report 2015. 2015.

Hamill, M., & Katerina, G. P. (2009). Common Trends in Software Fault and Failure Data. *IEEE Transactions on Software Engineering*, *35*(4), 484–496. doi:10.1109/TSE.2009.3

IEEE Computer Society Professional Practices Committee. (2014). *Guide to the Software Engineering Body of Knowledge (SWEBOK® Guide). Version 3.0*. IEEE.

Marasco, J. (2007). *"What Is the Cost of a Requirement Error?"* Stickyminds. Available at: https://www.stickyminds.com/article/what-cost-requirement-error

Pressman, R. S. (2014). *Software Engineering: A Practitioner's Approach* (8th ed.).

Spacey, J. (2016). *9 Examples of Positive Risk, 2016*. Available at: https://business.simplicable.com/business/new/9-examples-of-positive-risk

Chapter 5
Agile Team Measurement to Review the Performance in Global Software Development

Chamundeswari Arumugam
SSN College of Engineering, India

Srinivasan Vaidyanathan
Cognizant Technology Solutions, India

ABSTRACT

This chapter is aimed at studying the key performance indicators of team members working in an agile project environment and in an extreme programming software development. Practitioners from six different XP projects were selected to respond to the survey measuring the performance indicators, namely, escaped defects, team member's velocity, deliverables, and extra efforts. The chapter presents a comparative view of Scrum and XP, the two renowned agile methods with their processes, methodologies, development cycles, and artifacts, while assessing the base performance indicators in XP setup. These indicators are key to any agile project in a global software development environment. The observed performance indicators were compared against the gold standard industry benchmarks along with best, average, and worst-case scenarios. Practitioners from six agile XP projects were asked to participate in the survey. Observed results best serve the practitioners to take necessary course corrections to stay in the best-case scenarios of their respective projects.

DOI: 10.4018/978-1-5225-9659-2.ch005

INTRODUCTION

The software organization has completely moved on to Global Software Development(GSD) (Chamundeswari, Srinivasan & Harini, 2018) as its tends to improve the productivity, in spite of the risk they undergo in terms of the practitioners, environment, culture, etc. Organization gives more priorities to these mainly for cost reduction. Practitioners also on their part has many risk to undergo to take up assignment in this GSD, but in spite of it they take up the assignment because of the money, relocation, etc. This software development practice undergo four stages (Pressman, 2005), such as forming, stroming, norming and performing. Stage by stage the project progresses as a team for the product delivery. Due to agile approach the project team members can also progress in their skills to produce the best in them.

Though agile practices are many, taking the widely used aspect into concern, scrum and extreme programming is concentrated in this work. Agile, a Scrum process model (Bertrand, 2018) follow sprints or iteration to deliver a product. As the iteration flows it enables the customer to update their feedback and gets linked to next iteration delivery. Thus the incremental delivery for each iteration or sprint is achieved by this model. The team members co-operate to deliver the product in sprint as the project progress. Scrum has many key role members to execute a project development. It includes product owner, scrum master and team members. Each member has a role and task to be get committed on based on onsite or offshore project.

Extreme Programming (XP) is another agile framework that is widely used to produce high quality software by ensuring ease of development and quality of life for the team. XP is suitable when software requirements change dynamically, new technology is involved in a definitive timeline projects, team needs to be collocated for extended development, the selected technology lends itself for automated tests. It revolves around simplicity, communication, respect, courage and feedback. From a communication perspective, XP stresses on face to face communication through collocated teams. Simplicity involves keeping the design, coding simple so as to maintain easier support and revisions. Courage denotes bold decisions to doing what is right in the face of fear. Respect means demanding respect among the team members to freely give and accept feedback. In the feedback principle, teams identify areas of improvements and implement best practices.

The focus of the proposed work is inclined to analyze the key performance measure team members working in an Agile project environment in a Global Software Development(GSD)environment. Vital parameters that are important for the practitioners in various projects were chosen to survey the analyzes. Software production divisions follow many methodologies for GSD. Some organization follow scrum 100% while other follow extreme programming. Still it is open to follow any approach as far as the organization has the culture and practices deployed for ease of the productivity. Now, in this chapter, the two popular agile approaches scrum and extreme programming is taken up for discussion in the context of GSD practitioners. In this work, influencing parameters taken up to measure team member performance in XP is discussed.

BACKGROUND

Diane et al. (2012) proved agile model increases co-ordination effectiveness. Meghann et al. (2012) worked on decision making principles in agile software development. Emily et al. (2013) investigated the team performance using the team factors. Fabian et al. (2014) suggested few factors to improve the developer's performance. Mikko et al. (2014) identified five communication wastes in global agile projects and how to mitigate them to increase development. Srikrishnan et al. (2014) highlighted the risk culture and practice in agile software development. Ashay et al. (2014) worked on the virtual team member contribution towards global projects. Georgieos et al. (2015) observation states agile improves employee and customer satisfaction.

Paul et al. (2015) concentrated on various aspects beyond technical skill sets for the project team members and listed 53 attributes to assess their performance. Rafael et al. (2016) proposed guidelines to improve development strategy for developing quality product using virtual team members. Serhat et al (2016) proposed eleven influencing factors and dependency among the factors with respect to global project team members. Ricardo et al. (2016) used stochastic automata networks (SAN) to study the coordination in distributed project for a specific project configuration. Rafael (2016) analysed the agile software development practices and observed that it makes a positive effect. Torgeir et al. (2014) assessed the co-located team performance that follows agile practices for development.

David et al. (2016) assessed the traditional and targeted scrum and confirmed that targeted scrum has no remarkable change in top and worst performing teams. Yngve et al. (2016) assessed and observed that agile development has only minimal variation with respect to traditional software team. Daniel et al. (2017) performed a survey and analyzed the unhappiness of the software developer. Suggested and recommended the means to improve the fall condition. Itanaua et al. (2017) identified psychological factors with team members in agile method and concluded that trust has more significant impact among team members. Lucas et al. (2017) proved the fact that group maturity in team agility has influence towards the contribution of product. Leo at al. (2016) remarked industry has high use of agile methodologies and also its factors has influence in software development.

Table 1. Literature survey comparison

Year	References	Comparison parameter	Number of authors (referred)
2012	[17]	Agile practices	6
2016	[22][15][9]		
2017	[6]		
2018	[10]		
2014	[18][28]	Risk	2
2000	[3]	Team Performance	18
2012	[17][7]		
2013	[11]		
2014	[1][12]		
2015	[13][19]		
2016	[21][27][25][29][9][30]		
2017	[8][14][16]		
2018	[23]		
2015	[13]	Customer satisfaction	1

Christof et. al. (2017) discusses the five agile framework and its adaption in industry for delivery. Dinesh (2018) explored the agile values and mentioned that the productivity increases by adapting this practice. Sadath et al. (2018) applied extreme programming in student projects to improve the learning capability, knowledge and skill of the students. Ramlall et al. (2018) studied the influence of personality traits of programmers when working from same and remote locations in Extreme programming. The literature survey reveals that many researchers have done performance measures on agile practices. But in this research work, the performance measures of two agile practices that is followed in the industry is explored and one of the measures is discussed in detail.

OVERVIEW

Agile methodology (2016) has many methods to adapt for software development. Notably Scrum, Extreme programming are the two different types of methods taken up in this work for performance measurement. Agile methodology, scrum in GSD projects has scrum master, product owner, and team members to play a vital role in development (2018). Product owner may be a business analyst or customer who is responsible for product backlog, while scrum master organizes sprint meeting

Figure 1. Scrum process

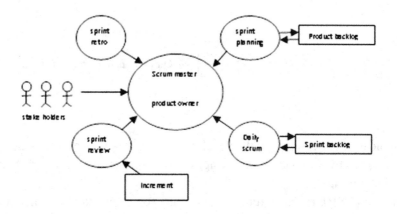

and responsible for sprint backlog. Product backlog has all feature information and sprint backlog has details about user stories and the delivery plan of various units in sprint. Team members split the tasks, in various sprint or iteration. Scrum block diagram is represented in Fig 1. It is expected that all team members complete the task without affecting business. But in normal scenario things may change.

Extreme programming (XP) is a well-known agile software development methodology created by Kent Beck (2000). XP is used for software development in various organization to produce high quality software with quality life for development team. XP is practiced because it follows five values, such as communication, simplicity, feedback, courage, and respect. Coding, testing, listening and designing are the four basic activities (SelectBS, n.d.) in this agile method. Customer or business analyst, who is a part of the team will jointly work with the developers. User stories of the customer requirements are delivered in short cycles of iteration and the stakeholder

Figure 2. XP process - collocated environment

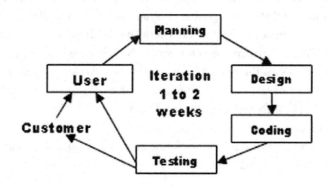

Figure 3. Difference between Scrum and XP

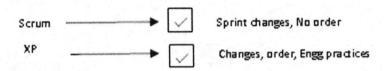

communicate their feedback to the developer for changes. To improve quality code, refactoring feature is enabled in testing. Extreme programming block diagram is represented in Fig 2.

Scrum and XP are quite aligned but there are some delicate differences between them (Differences, n.d.). Scrum work is in sprints, that last for 2 to 4 weeks. Whereas XP work in iterations that last for 1 to weeks. While Scrum product backlog items are packaged and committed into a Sprint, changes are not entertained throughout the sprint cycle, XP allows for changes in its iterations. If the work on a specific features hasn't started, a new feature can be substituted into its iteration in swap of the other feature. In XP, customer determines the order of the work to be executed, whereas SCRUM product owner determines order of priority in SCRUM and the team gets the flexibility of working in a sequence according to the project resources and code constraints. XP advocates engineering practices while SCRUM doesn't prescribe any. Simple design, Pair programming, test-driven development, refactoring and automated testing are some of the practices XP mandates. SCRUM doesn't mandate such practices rather let the team figure them out on their own. Figure 3. represents the differences between scrum and XP.

Agile Metrics

The success factor in GSD projects depends on the productive team members. Adapting XP practice and measuring the team members to study the progress of success rate in the organization is really challengeable. Already the KPI for agile scrum practice to measure the team member performance was defined (Chamundeswari, Sriraghav, & Baskaran, 2017) and here this measurement is compared with XP practice to study the resultant outcome of the two agile practices. The productive team members are the building blocks of the organization and the Key Performance Indicator (KPI) to measure them is discussed in Equation 1 to 4.

Escaped defects, a metrics to track the defects in the delivered product. It is essential to measure this metrics to apply the corrective steps at the early stage. The metric function F1, is stated in Equation 1.

Equation 1: Escaped defects$_{\text{iteration\#i}}$(F1) =

$$\frac{\text{No. of escaped defects in an iteration by a team member}}{\text{Total no. of escaped defects in an iteration}}$$

An iteration has many user stories, and each user stories has many tasks to which team members get committed in an iteration. Generally, each iteration may span to 1 to 2 weeks. The metric function F2, is stated in Equation 2.

Equation 2: Team member velocity$_{\text{iteration\#i}}$(F2) =

$$\frac{\text{No. of task completed by a team member in an iteration}}{\text{Total no. of committed tasks in an iteration}}$$

Deliverables metrics, measures actual hours taken by a team member in an iteration to complete a task from the total planned hours. The metric function F3, is stated is Equation 3.

Equation 3: Deliverables$_{\text{iteration\#i}}$(F3) =

$$\frac{\text{Actual hrs spent to complete committed task in an iteration}}{\text{Total planned hrs to complete committed task in an iteration}}$$

Extra effort spent by a member to develop defect free complete his task is an important metrics to measure the total effort spent to deliver a defect free product. The metrics function F4, is given in Equation 4.

Equation 4: Extra Effort$_{\text{sprint\#i}}$ (F4) =

$$\frac{\text{Extra hrs worked to fix bugs in an iteration by a team member}}{\text{Actual hrs spent to complete committed task in an iteration} + \text{Extra hours}}$$

RESULTS AND DISCUSSION

Four defined metrics in Section 4 are assessed by framing seven questions to extract the response from practitioners, following the context given in this work. Table 2. represents the questions framed to extract the answers for the metrics defined in Section "Agile Metrics". Judgmental or purposive sampling was done in identifying the projects for participation in the survey. The practitioners were chosen from 6 different IT companies who executed Agile XP projects. Anonymity of data was ensured prior to analyzing and interpreting the results.

Seven survey questions were framed for the four metrics defined. Survey questionnaire was circulated to the identified practitioners, practicing the agile extreme programming for their projects in their respective organizations. Metrics data along with industry bench mark (Chamundswari et al., 2018), best, average, and worst case is represented in Table 3.

It is identified that the 5 project metrics out of 6 projects is measurable and only one project data, project 3 is not correct. Project 1, 2, 4, 5 and 6 were measurable. The graph was plotted with collected data and represented in Fig. 4. From the graph, it is observed that the P1 and P2 has some worst case scenario and need focus on the software practitioners who are involved in development.

Table 2. Survey questions for defined metrics.

Metrics	Survey questions
F1	• How many defects likely occur in your task per iteration ? • How many defects likely occur by all team members in a project per iteration ?
F2	• Quantify the tasks committed in a project per iteration. • Quantify the tasks you complete in an iteration.
F3	• What is the actual hours taken to complete your committed task in an iteration? • What is the planned hours to complete committed task in an iteration?
F4	• Did you took extra hours to fix bugs in your committed task in an iteration ?
-	• Feedback about the survey.

Table 3. Metrics data

Metrics	Project 1 (P1)	Project 2 (P2)	Project 3 (P3)	Project 4 (P4)	Project 5 (P5)	Project 6 (P6)
F1	0.1(best case)	0.2(avg case)	0.3(avg case)	0(best case)	0.3(avg case)	0.25(best case)
F2	0.1(worst case)	0.375(worst case)	0.3(worst case)	1 (best case)	1 (best case)	1(best case)
F3	1(best case)	1.2(best case)	10	0.8(avg case)	1(best case)	1(best case)
F4	0.16(best case)	0.05(best case)	0.25(avg case)	0(best case)	0(best case)	0(best case)

FUTURE RESEARCH DIRECTIONS

As a future extension, with a larger sample base, AI based clustering and prediction algorithms can be leveraged in grouping the inputs and predicting the output respectively based on historical data patterns. Future researchers can assume and study the effect of additional performance indicators for empirical analysis from both Scrum and XP perspectives to verify the consistency of results. Also, the study can be repeated with projects of varying degrees of complexity and observe results. Finally the study can also be repeated for varying scopes of the projects and technological implementations, may it be legacy, new or digital technologies.

CONCLUSION

This chapter has taken a plunge into the set of base performance indicators to measure the team performance and act upon the right signals on a XP project. Practitioners from six Agile XP projects in IT industry participated in the survey. From the preliminary data analysis, Project 3's data weren't measurable and hence was discarded. Other set of projects' data were subjected to detailed analysis and it was concluded that:

- The performance metric "Team Member Velocity" needed focus for the practitioners of Projects 1 and 2. They need to implement substantial changes to the committed total number of tasks in an iteration and the number of tasks completed by the team members in that iteration. That will help them

Figure 4. Metrics data representation

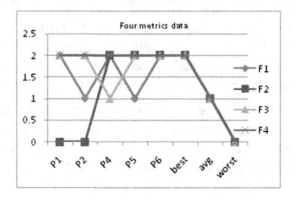

to improve from worst case to the best case scenario to stay aligned with industry benchmarks.

- The performance metric "Escaped Defects" needed focus for the practitioners of Projects 2 and 5. They need to implement moderate changes to the escaped total number of defects in an iteration and the number of escaped defects by the team members in that iteration. That will help them to improve from average case to the best case scenario to stay aligned with industry benchmarks.

- The performance meric "Deliverables" needed focus for the practitioner of Project 4. The practitioner needs to implement moderate changes to the planned total number of hours to complete committed tasks in an iteration and the actual number of hours spent by the team members in that iteration. That will help to improve from average case to the best case scenario to stay aligned with industry benchmarks.

Observed results best serve the practitioners to take necessary course corrections to stay in the best case scenarios of their respective projects. The study also proves the point that while Scrum and XP are two different agile methodologies, the base performance indicators to measure the project and team members productivity are applicable to both.

REFERENCES

Ashay, S., & Johanna, B. (2014). Factors affecting team performance in globally distributed setting. *Proceedings of the 52nd ACM conference on Computers and people research*, 25-33.

Beck, K. (2000). *Extreme Programming Explained: Embrace Change*. Reading, MA: Addison Wesley Longman, Inc.

Bertrand, M. (2018). Making Sense of Agile Methods. *IEEE Software*, 91–94.

Chamundeswari, A., Srinivasan, V., & Harini, K. (2018). Global Software Development: Key Performance Measures of Team in a SCRUM based Agile Environment. In *19th International Conference on Computational Science and Applications, Proceedings published in Springer LNCS*. Monash University.

Chamundeswari, A., Sriraghav, K., & Baskaran, K. (2017). Global Software Development:A design framework to measure the risk of the global practitioners. In *ACM International Conference on Computer and Communication Technology*. Motilal Nehru National Institute of Technology.

Christof, E., & Maria, P. (2017). Scaling Agile. *IEEE Software*, 98–103.

Daniel, G., Fabian, F., Xiaofeng, W., & Pekka, A. (2017). Consequences of unhappiness while developing software. *Proceedings of the 2nd International Workshop on Emotion Awareness in Software Engineering*, 42-47.

David, P. H., & Arvin, A. (2016). Targeted Scrum: Applying Mission Command to Agile Software Development. *IEEE Transactions on Software Engineering*, *42*(5), 476–489. doi:10.1109/TSE.2015.2489654

Diane, E. S., Sid, L. H., Beverley, H., & Sebastian, L. (2012). Coordination in co-located agile software development projects. *Journal of Systems and Software*, *85*(6), 1222–1238. doi:10.1016/j.jss.2012.02.017

Differences Between Scrum And Extreme Programming. (n.d.). Retrieved from https://www.mountaingoatsoftware.com/blog/differences-between-scrum-and-extreme-programming

Dinesh, B. (2018). Agile values or plan-driven aspects: Which factor contributes more toward the success of data warehousing, business intelligence, and analytics project development? *Journal of Systems and Software*, *146*, 249–262. doi:10.1016/j.jss.2018.09.081

Emily, W., Ariadi, N., Joost, V., & Aske, P. (2013). Towards high performance software teamwork. *Proceedings of the 17th International Conference on Evaluation and Assessment in Software Engineering*, 212-215.

Fabian, F., Marko, I., Petri, K., Jürgen, M., Virpi, R., & Pekka, A. (2014). How do software developers experience team performance in lean and agile environments? *Proceedings of the 18th International Conference on Evaluation and Assessment in Software Engineering*.

Georgios, P. (2015). Moving from traditional to agile software development methodologies also on large, distributed projects. *Procedia: Social and Behavioral Sciences*, *175*, 455–463. doi:10.1016/j.sbspro.2015.01.1223

Itanauã, F. B., Marcela, P. O., Priscila, B. S. R., Tancicleide, C. S. G., & Fabio, Q. B. D. S. (2017). Towards understanding the relationships between interdependence and trust in software development: a qualitative research. *10th International Workshop on Cooperative and Human Aspects of Software Engineering*, 66-69.

Leo, R. V., & Charles, W. B. (2016). Choice of Software Development Methodologies Do Organizational, Project, and Team Characteristics Matter? *IEEE Software*, 86–94.

Lucas, G., Richard, T., & Robert, F. (2017). Group development and group maturity when building agile teams: A qualitative and quantitative investigation at eight large companies. *Journal of Systems and Software, 124*, 104–119. doi:10.1016/j.jss.2016.11.024

Meghann, D., Kieran, C., & Ken, P. (2012). Obstacles to decision making in Agile software development teams. *Journal of Systems and Software, 85*(6), 1239–1254. doi:10.1016/j.jss.2012.01.058

Mikko, K., & Frank, M. (2014). Waste identification as the means for improving communication in globally distributed agile software development. *Journal of Systems and Software, 95*, 122–140. doi:10.1016/j.jss.2014.03.080

Paul, L., Andrew, J. K., & Jiamin, Z. (2015). What makes a great software engineer? *37th International Conference on Software Engineering*, 700-710.

Pressman, R. (2005). *Software Engineering: A Practitioner's Approach*. McGraw-Hill.

Rafael, P., Casper, L., Evelyn, T., & Jeffrey, C. C. (2016). Trends in Agile Perspectives from the Practitioners. *IEEE Software*, 20–22.

Rafael, P., Marcelo, P., & Sabrina, M. (2016). Virtual Team Configurations that Promote Better Product Quality. *Proceedings of the 10th ACM/IEEE International Symposium on Empirical Software Engineering and Measurement*.

Ramlall, P., & Chuttur, M. Y. (2018). An Experimental Study to Investigate Personality Traits on Pair Programming Efficiency in Extreme Programming. *5th International Conference on Industrial Engineering and Applications*, 95 - 99.

Ricardo, B., Darja, Š., & Lars-Ola, D. (2016). Experiences from Measuring Learning and Performance in Large-Scale Distributed Software Development. *Proceedings of the 10th ACM/IEEE International Symposium on Empirical Software Engineering and Measurement*.

Ricardo, M.C., Paulo, F., Lucelene, L., Afonso, S., Alan R. S., & Thais, W. (2016). Stochastic Performance Analysis of Global Software Development Teams. *ACM Transactions on Software Engineering and Methodology, 25*(3), 26:1-26:32.

Sadath, L., Karim, K., & Gill, S. (2018). Extreme programming implementation in academia for software engineering sustainability. *International Conference on Advances in Science and Engineering Technology*, 1-6. 10.1109/ICASET.2018.8376925

Serhat, S., Ramazan, K., & Bulent, S. (2016). Factors Affecting Multinational Team Performance. *Procedia: Social and Behavioral Sciences, 25*(3), 60–69.

Srikrishnan, S., Marath, B., & Pramod, K. V. (2014). Case study on risk management practice in large offshore-outsourced Agile software projects. *IET Software*, *8*(6), 245–257. doi:10.1049/iet-sen.2013.0190

Torgeir, D., Tor, E. F., Tore, D., Børge, H., & Yngve, L. (2016). Team Performance in Software Development Research Results versus Agile Principles. *IEEE Software*, 106–110.

What Is Extreme Programming? (XP). (n.d.). Retrieved from http://www.selectbs.com/process-maturity/what-is-extreme-programming

Yngve, L., Dag, I. K. S., Torgeir, D., Gunnar, R. B., & Tore, D. (2016). Teamwork quality and project success in software development: A survey of agile development teams. *Journal of Systems and Software*, *122*, 274–286. doi:10.1016/j.jss.2016.09.028

ADDITIONAL READING

Saru, D., Deepak, K., & Singh, V. B. (2018). Success and Failure Factors that Impact on Project Implementation Using Agile Software Development Methodology. *Software Engineering. Springer AISC.*, *731*, 647–654.

Chapter 6
Improving Construction Management Through Advanced Computing and Decision Making

Varun Gupta
University of Beira Interior, Covilha, Portugal

Aditya Raj Gupta
Amity University, Noida, India

Utkarsh Agrawal
Amity University, Noida, India

Ambika Kumar
Amity University, Noida, India

Rahul Verma
Amity University, Noida, India

ABSTRACT

This chapter proposes an algorithm to make the bidding dynamic by not only awarding tenders on basis of cost quoted in tenders (biding cost) but also on contractor ratings. The ratings of contractors are computed using historical performance of contractor. The chapter empirically identifies the factors to rate the contractors. The historical values associated with the performance rating parameters are then combined using the "controlled values" which one assumed to standard across the industry, to yield the overall weighted rating of firms. This rating is then combined with the bidding cost, thereby making the selection of contractor dynamic. The selected contractor is paid bidding cost. The algorithm is executed a hypothetical value to illustrate the approach. A web-based tool had been proposed to automate the process of making the bidding dynamic.

DOI: 10.4018/978-1-5225-9659-2.ch006

INTRODUCTION

There are several civil contractors in the market who competes for a tender. Usually, the contractor who puts up the lowest cost bid gets the tender. But this sometimes reduces the quality of the product in favor of cost reduction. So, there is a need for a more refined process so that the best contractor can be selected, offering economical cost services for the project without compromising with the quality. Therefore, an optimal method is required that makes the selection of contractor not only on the basis of given cost but also on his past performance. Past performance calculation will be a dynamic & continuous process and is computed by employing historical values of various parameters, as identified empirically in this paper. This performance is the representation of the rating of the contractor, which is used to normalize bid cost to yield priority among competing contractors. The parameters used for rating the contractor varies from firm to firm. However, the various parameters are reported in (Xie, Lin, Yang, & Gao, 2008; Watt, Kavis & Willey, 2010; Hassaan, Fors & Sheata, 2013; Ibadoy, 2015; Arujo, Alencar & Mota, 2018) and could be used with the algorithm proposed in the chapter.

Proposed Algorithm

The proposed algorithm will give the ranking of a contractor. This ranking will help in reducing the cost of the project and selects the contractor whose history of work is also good i.e. has all the values that are required to complete a particular project. The parameters range with different values are set by the company that puts the project. Also, these parameters are known in the industry.

A suitable contractor would be selected on the basis of lowest bid value and highest ranking i.e. Priority of a contractor = Rating/ Bidding Cost. There are two new terms introduced, the contractor cost which is the cost given by a contractor to win the bidding and control points which are the standard values known across the industry but unknown to a contractor. Control values are given to select the right contractor on the basis of his historical values. The rating is generated by taking various primary and secondary parameters whose values are dependent on historical records of a contractor.

In the calculation of rating, density is calculated for each parameter with the help of historical values. Density is the total number of points in a control rectangle upon the total area of the control rectangle. The steps to calculate the density for each parameter are:

1. Create a graph, Parameter (Y – axis) - Time (X- axis)
2. Plot historical values of a firm on graph.

3. Draw control rectangle on the basis of the coordinates which are fixed values for the selection of a contractor.
4. Calculate the density.
5. Calculate priority using formulae (1).

$$Priority = Rating / Bidding\ Cost \tag{1}$$

In order to calculate the overall rating, densities of individual parameters are multiplied to the weights of each parameter. Weights are given to indicate the importance if a parameter. Primary parameter would have higher weight value as compared to the second parameter.

$$Rating = W_1(D_1) + W_2(D_2) + \ldots\ldots + W_n(D_n), \tag{2}$$

where W is the weight and D is the density of each parameter.

Hypothetical Example

It is assumed that "n" number of contractor can fill tender for a project and "n" number of contractors are eligible for bidding. Suppose, in a bid, there are three contractors A, B and C. Out of which C has taken no project before, so its rating would not be possible to determine. Since C too is eligible to participate in the bidding, C can undertake a joint project with any other high ranking contractor. This will increase C's chances of getting selected as a contractor. Also there are five parameters, each with different historical points are considered, as given below (Table 1).

In this, the X and Y axis are taken from range 0 to 9, for the sake of uniform calculations of all parameters and the coordinates for the control rectangle are provided by the firm. It is also assumed that all the contractor give the same amount for the completion of the project. Now to determine the best contractor for the project, rating becomes a crucial factor.

Table 1. Historical points

	Weight	Total No. of Points for A	Total No. of Points for B	Total No. of Points for C
Parameter E	5	12	4	7
Parameter F	4	7	5	5
Parameter G	3	6	5	8
Parameter H	2	5	5	11
Parameter I	1	3	7	4

When these three contractors bid against each other, the density of each parameter is calculated and that is multiplied with the weight of each parameter and it's shown that the second contractor wins the bidding as his rating is higher than the rest.

Since this is a dynamic and continuous process, the rating is always affected by the completion of each project. This is done by another factor, a credit system that is valid, which will automatically add the values of different parameters at the end.

Company A

Density= No of points in control graph/ Area of Control Graph
Density= 12/11.85=1.012
Density=No of points in control graph/Area of Control Graph Density=7/6.71=1.0432
Density=No of points in control graph/ Area of Control Graph Density=6/5.6=1.0714
Density=No of points in control graph/ Area of Control Graph Density=5/6=0.8333
Density= No of points in control graph/ Area of Control Graph Density=3/1=3

Figure 1. Density of Parameter E for Company A

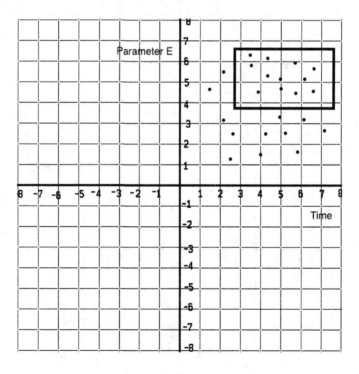

Figure 2. Density of Parameter F for Company A

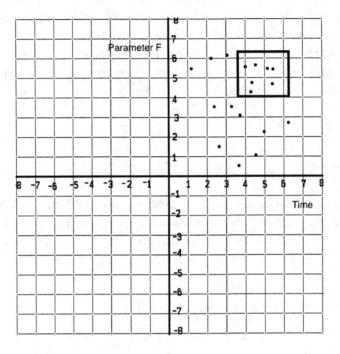

Figure 3. Density of Parameter G for Company A

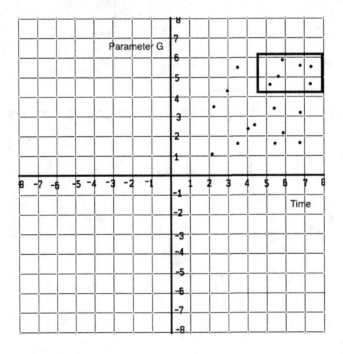

Figure 4. Density of Parameter H for Company A

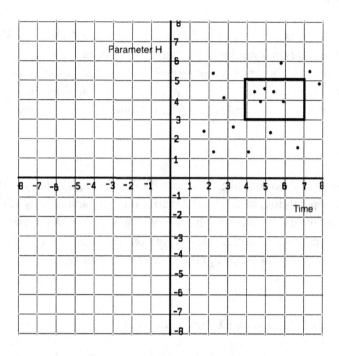

Figure 5. Density of Parameter I for Company A

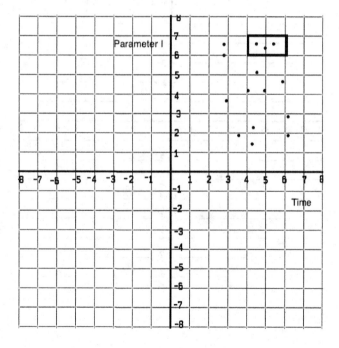

Company B

Density= No of points in control graph/ Area of Control Graph Density=4/1.87=2.139
Density= No of points in control graph / Area of Control Graph Density=5/2.8=1.7857
Density= No of points in control graph/ Area of Control Graph Density=5/5.6=0.899
Density= No of points in control graph/ Area of Control Graph Density=5/8.4=0.5952
Density= No of points in control graph/ Area of Control Graph Density=7/5.54=1.26

Company C

Density= No of points in control graph/ Area of Control Graph Density=7/6.12=1.143
Density= No of points in control graph/ Area of Control Graph Density=5/1.69=2.958
Density= No of points in control graph/ Area of Control Graph Density=8/5.92=1.351
Density= No of points in control graph/ Area of Control Graph Density=11/6.3=1.7460
Density= No of points in control graph/ Area of Control Graph.
Density =4/3.12=1.282

Figure 6. Density of Parameter E for Company B

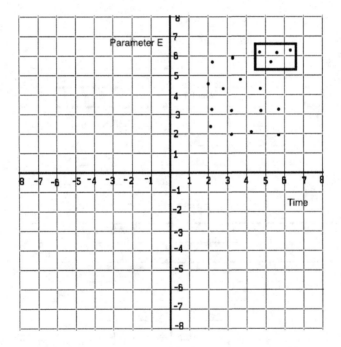

Figure 7. Density of Parameter F for Company B

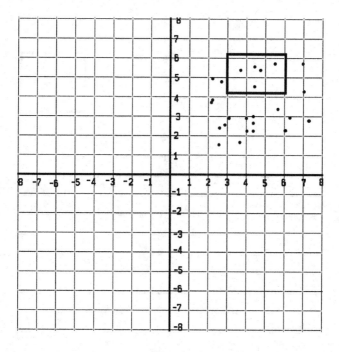

Figure 8. Density of Parameter G for Company B

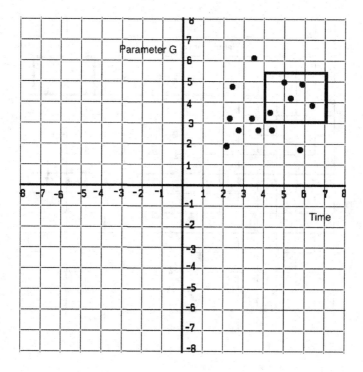

Figure 9. Density of Parameter H for Company B

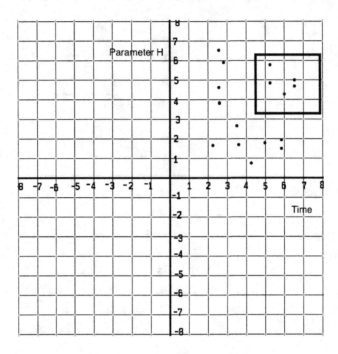

Figure 10. Density of Parameter I for Company B

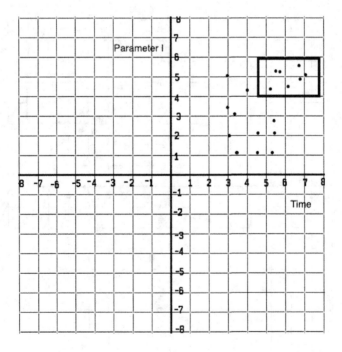

Figure 11. Density of Parameter E for Company C

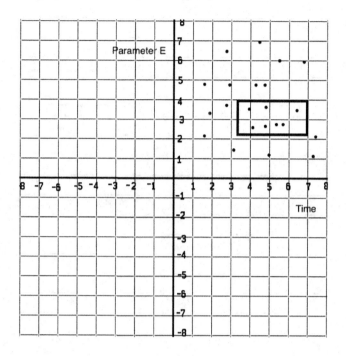

Figure 12.Density of Parameter F for Company C

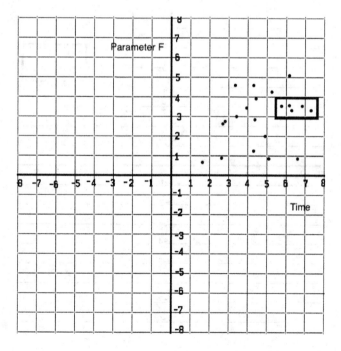

Figure 13. Density of Parameter G for Company C

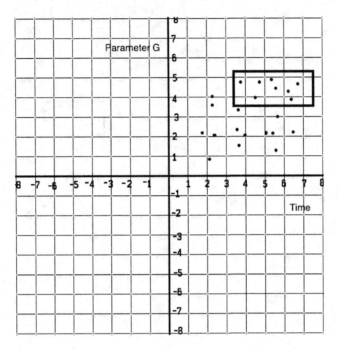

Figure 14. Density of Parameter H for Company C

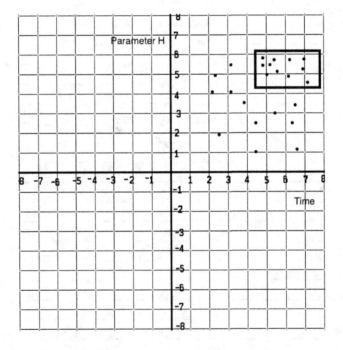

Figure 15. Density of Parameter I for Company C

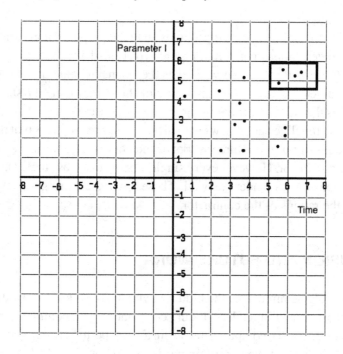

Calculations

Ratings

Company A- 1.012*5+1.0432*4+1.0714*3+0.8333*2+3*1=17.1136
Company B- 2.139*5+1.7857*4+0.899*3+0.5952*2+1.26*1=22.9852
Company C- 1.143*5+2.958*4+1.351*3+1.7460*2+1.282*1=26.374

Priority

Bidding cost of A=150
Bidding cost of B=180
Bidding cost of C=230
Priority(A)=17.1136/150=0.1140
Priority(B)=22.9852/180=0.12769
Priority(B)=26.3740/230=0.11466

Result is that, the priority of B is highest among the three so B is the winner here.

Tool Support

A web application has been developed to execute the proposed algorithm. The web application screen shots are given in Figures 16 ,17 and 18.

Figure 16 shows that the software takes the financial value of the contractor as an initial parameter for assigning the rating of the firm. Figure 17 shows that the software takes the values of previous three works of the contractor and adds them to rating based on timeline and reviews in certificate. Figure 18 shows that the software takes the values of on going three works of the contractor and further adds to the rating of the contractor. However every single work is taken as single entity and can be optional for various tenders as well. These parameters are generic parameters that affects the ratings of the contractor.

CONCLUSION AND FUTURE WORK

The proposed algorithm makes the bidding dynamic by not only awarding tenders on basis of cost quoted in tenders (biding cost) but also on contractor ratings. The ratings of contractor is computed using historical performance of contractor. It could be concluded that the algorithm needs to be enough scalable to work as per the parameters defining rating of the contractor. Further, tt is also to be noted that in order to select the contractor, the control points would be given by the company that has the project to ensure the fair selection of a contractor. The selection must be therefore based on objective judgments. Validation of the proposed structure is kept as future work.

Figure 16. Financial parameter as ratting factor.

Figure 17. Previous projects values as rating factors.

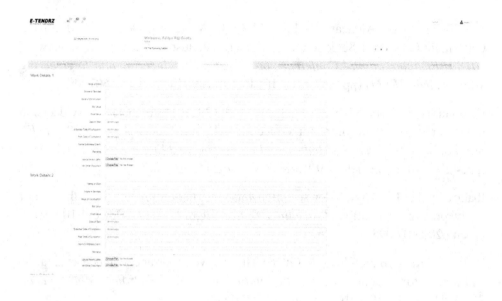

Figure 18. Values of ongoing projects as rating parameters.

There are many features that can be added to the web application developed so that the application can be a standalone application for all the process of e tendering and the selection of the bidder. The current algorithms can be further more refined in order to make the algorithm work more efficiently.

REFERENCES

Araújo, M. C. B., Alencar, L. H., & Mota, C. M. (2018, December). Decision Criteria for Contractor Selection in Construction Industry: A Literature Review. In *2018 IEEE International Conference on Industrial Engineering and Engineering Management (IEEM)* (pp. 637-640). IEEE. 10.1109/IEEM.2018.8607809

Hassaan, H. S., Fors, M. N., & Shehata, M. S. (2013, December). Fuzzy decision model for construction contractor's selection in Egypt: Tender phase. In *2013 IEEE International Conference on Industrial Engineering and Engineering Management* (pp. 420-426). IEEE. 10.1109/IEEM.2013.6962446

Ibadov, N. (2015). Contractor selection for construction project, with the use of fuzzy preference relation. *Procedia Engineering, 111*, 317–323. doi:10.1016/j.proeng.2015.07.095

Watt, D. J., Kayis, B., & Willey, K. (2010). The relative importance of tender evaluation and contractor selection criteria. *International Journal of Project Management, 28*(1), 51–60. doi:10.1016/j.ijproman.2009.04.003

Xie, X. M., Lin, J. Y., Yang, G., & Gao, J. (2008, October). Research on Contractor Selection of Telecommunication Project. In *2008 4th International Conference on Wireless Communications, Networking and Mobile Computing* (pp. 1-7). IEEE. 10.1109/WiCom.2008.2464

Chapter 7
An Investigation on Quality Perspective of Software Functional Artifacts

Vimaladevi M.
Pondicherry Engineering College, Puducherry, India

Zayaraz G.
Pondicherry Engineering College, Puducherry, India

ABSTRACT

Software engineering process and practices paramount the crisis of cost, quality, and schedule constraints in developing software products. This chapter surveys the quality improvement techniques for the two fundamental artifacts of software product development, namely the architecture design and the source code. The information from top level research databases are compiled and an overall picture of quality enhancement in current software trends during the design, development, and maintenance phases are presented. This helps both the software developers and the quality analysts to gain understanding of the current state of the art for quality improvement of design and source code and the usage of various practices. The results indicate the need for more realistic, precise, automated technique for architectural quality analysis. The complex nature of the current software products requires the system developed to be beyond robust and resilient and building intelligent software that is anti-fragile and self-adaptive is favored. Innovative proposals that reduce the cost and time are invited.

DOI: 10.4018/978-1-5225-9659-2.ch007

INTRODUCTION

Software Engineering has emerged legitimately in developing high quality software products right from its inception. The discipline of Software Engineering evolved over the past 70 years shaping its key activities providing a framework to the stakeholders to structure, plan, develop and control the software development process. The origin of software engineering dates back to 1950s, where the initial crisis was productivity and now it has evolved to quality. Software quality assessment and improvement is a vast area of research and many techniques and processes are proposed for quality improvement in various stages of the software life cycle. Any quality assurance technique strives to achieve zero errors post release. In spite of all these constant and effective techniques, there are still some failures in the software that makes the software difficult to survive. Irrespective of the type of software and the technology used in development, all software products face the challenges in incorporating high quality within the cost and time constraints. There are multiple definitions of Quality such as conformance to requirements, satisfying customer needs, achieving zero defects, etc. Software applications are becoming more complex day by day and it is difficult to maintain code quality that make the Quality-Cost balance a challenging task.

The study reported in this work will lay a foundation of quality needs and various strategies available that the stakeholders may select to build high quality software products considering the design architectures and the source code. It is mandatory to evaluate a software quality and the quality assessment has to be performed in parallel with the software development. Every industry is now computerized and is used in critical areas where quality becomes a key factor to ensure successful business and human safety. Software is becoming more and more complex and it is mandatory to select, apply and evaluate relevant techniques and processes to keep the risks low. Evaluation has to be done in order to understand a software product. Understanding involves testing of software whether it is easy to use, hard to modify, can be integrated with other programs, etc.

There exists a vast set of literature that discuss about software quality. They focus on a specific phase of a software development or adhere to certain techniques and tools. This work in contrast to the existing literature reviews; the quality aspects taking the two major artifacts of the software development are studied. They are the Architectural Design and the Source Code. All the Software Engineering principles, process models, quality frameworks, testing tools and techniques are aimed in fulfilling the user requirements and thus achieved desired quality. Even though the software development process generates different artifacts at different phases, all that is used to increase the quality of the developed source code. The quality of the source code is directly related to the design choices made during the analysis and the design phase. Hence, in contrast to the existing literature focusing of a particular phase or an artifact, this work discusses the quality improvement methods available for evaluating the design documents and the source code of an Object Oriented Software System.

Any software irrespective of the type, size, and technology goes through a series of phases as described in the life cycle models. There are five basic phases for the software development process. They are Planning & Analysis, Design, Development, Testing and Maintenance. The planning and analysis phase is involved in studying the scope of the project, understanding the requirements, planning the deliverables, cost estimates, etc. The design phase builds the architecture of the project and the development phase is where the actual product is coded and built. The testing phases assess the software for bugs next to which the software progresses to the maintenance phase. During maintenance, the software is maintained and upgraded from time to time for any changes. The quality activity of the software starts at the very early stages of planning where the deliverables and the quality control activities are finalized. Every artifact produced during the software development goes through a quality check process.

Testing is viewed as the phase where the quality of the software is drastically improved. There are different types and techniques available for executing the testing process. One of the major overhead in software development is cost of testing and bug fixing and this cost increases exponentially in later phases. The software bug cost of United States economy has increased from $59.5 billion to $1.1 trillion from 2002 to 2016. This increase in cost is due to the loss in revenue due to the software being unusable, payments to developers for bug fixing, loss in shareholder value, etc. Also, there are some indirect financial costs arising due to the problem of brand reputation and customer loyalty. The bug fixing process even interferes with other developments and enhancements for new functionality addition that ultimately affect the project schedule. From the report of National Institute of Standards and Technology (NIST), the increase in the bug fix follows the trend as shown in Table 1 (National Institute of Standards and Technology, 2002). Here, X is the normalized unit of cost and can be expressed in terms of person-hours.

The most effective way to keep the development cost down is the minimization and the introduction of defects. In order to achieve this, care need to be taken to assess and improve design quality. Also, quality has be considered prime factor right from the requirements and analysis phase and not be emphasized only during testing and maintenance phases. Hence, the software developed should incorporate some mechanism to develop and improve quality along with fulfilling the functional needs of the software. This chapter discusses about the characteristic the software should possess, which is not documented in the requirements specification. The following sections introduce the key concepts of quality models, quality attributes,

Table 1. Cost of Bug Fixing

Phase	Cost estimate
Design	1X
Implementation	5 X
Integration Testing	10 X
Customer Beta Testing	15 X
Post Product Release	30 X

software architecture, software architecture analysis techniques, characteristics of source code desired, and the techniques to improve the quality of the developed source code using refactoring. Notable works from major databases such as IEEE, Elsevier, Springer, and Association for Computing Machinery (ACM) are referenced.

SOFTWARE QUALITY REQUIREMENTS

The definition of software quality provided by IEEE (IEEE, 1991) is mentioned below.
   Software quality is:

1.   The degree to which a system, component, or process meets specified requirements.
2.   The degree to which a system, component, or process meets customer or user needs or expectations.

   The quality definition is stated in simple terms but the process to achieve bulletin it is slightly tricky, demanding the usage of quality processes and techniques. Multiple works have been published by the research community striving to achieve this stated quality. Software Quality Models are proposed to understand and evaluate the quality needs of software against a set of general or specific criteria. Popular quality models include Boehm, McCall, FURPS, Dromey (Al-Badareen, Selamat, Jabar, Din, & Turaev, 2011; Miguel, Mauricio, & Rodríguez, 2014) and ISO/IEC 9126 (ISO/IEC TR 9126-2, 2003) replaced by ISO/IEC 25010:2011 (ISO/IEC, 2011). These models define the quality of software on the basis of a set of credentials or measurements for certain quality characteristics called the quality attributes. Some of the important quality attributes are defined below.

- *Maintainability* is the ease with which the product can be maintained. Maintenance includes situations like correcting the software for bugs, updating for new requirements, and cope with the changes environment.
- *Reliability* refers to the failure free operation of software for a specified period of time in a specified environment.
- *Flexibility* refers to that attribute of the software that can adapt to external changes and how it responds to uncertainty.
- *Testability* attribute refers to the degree to which a software component supports testing. This makes uncovering the bugs easier.
- *Portability* measures how easily the same software can be used in a different environment with minimal changes.
- *Usability* refers to how efficiently and effectively the software can be used by the human community.
- *Efficiency* refers to the performance of the software utilizing minimal resources and maximizing the output.
- *Reusability* refers to the reuse of existing software artifacts in various formats. This is helpful to overcome the software crisis in a cost-effective manner.

The Architectural Design Quality

The Bass, Clements, and Kazman definition of architecture (Bass, Clements, & Kazman 2013) is stated as:

"The software architecture of a program or computing system is the structure or structures of the system, which comprise software elements, the externally visible properties of those elements, and the relationships among them. Architecture is concerned with the public side of interfaces; private details of elements—details having to do solely with internal implementation—are not architectural."

During the design phase, the quality analysis is done from the architecture diagrams. This artifact consists of primarily the Class Diagrams for predicting the quality. The Unified Modeling Language (UML) is a standard modeling language used by the software engineering community to represent, visualize, construct and document the software artifacts. UML provides a set of diagrams to represent the architecture of the product under construction. Class diagrams are central component of design which is a pictorial representation of the relationships and the dependencies available in the software source code. During the design phase, class diagrams are developed by grouping similar objects that are identified from the requirements of the software. In most of the projects, especially during the initial design phases, the Class diagrams developed lack complete information due to some ambiguity that may exist in the requirements specifications and also as a result of complex nature of the objects. These vagueness and incompleteness has to be resolved in the later phases during the course of the software development. Hence, there is a need to do an initial assessment of the software quality such as maintainability and reliability with the initial Class diagrams generated even in the presence of such vagueness. A fuzzy UML representation can be used to overcome such ambiguities. Zhou et al. (2009), explain the fuzzy UML logistics that model the real world uncertain, vague and fuzzy information using a semi-formed Fuzzy UML. Fuzzy Classes, fuzzy generalization, fuzzy associations and fuzzy aggregations are illustrated. Ma, Zhang, and Yan (2011), introduces different levels of fuzziness in UML based on the fuzzy sets and possibility distribution theory and extends UML to Fuzzy UML data model. A formal mapping of this fuzzy UML to fuzzy relational database scheme is proposed. The fuzzy UML classes and the relationships such as Fuzzy Generalization Fuzzy Aggregation Fuzzy Association Fuzzy Dependency discussed are used to overcome the uncertainty that exists during the early design of the object oriented software.

Another important factor in quality assessment using software architecture is the choice of representational model of the architecture. There are various techniques that are available for the quality evaluation depending upon the choice of the representation model selected. Some of the modeling types available in the literature include DTMC (Discrete Time Markov Chain), CTMC (Continuous Time Markov Chain), SMP (Semi-Markov Process), Poisson Process, CDG (Component Dependency Graphs), Stochastic Petri Nets, Bayesian Networks and Complex Networks. These representational models assessed by the research community are discussed below.

Wang, Pan, and Chen (2006), discusses a method to estimate the reliability of a software using the architectural information of the Software and the Reliability models for decision making and quality control of the software. The white-box based models are used for decision making in the early phases of the software, whereas a black-box based model can be used in the later phases. This work considers the use a white-box based model extended to utilize the architectural styles and the heterogeneous behavior of the software systems. The model chosen for representation of the software architecture is a Discrete-Time Markov Chain (DTMC) Model. A Markov model is a finite state machine with probabilities for each transition, and a transition probability to the next state will depend on the current state only. For a discrete-time Markov model, the transitions occur only at discrete intervals of time or at discrete events, and the transition probabilities follow a discrete distribution.

In (Sharma & Trivedi, 2006), the authors propose architecture based unified hierarchical model for Reliability, Performance, Security, Cache behavior prediction in the same model. This approach facilitates the identification of various bottlenecks for Component based software. This work uses Discrete Time Markov Chains as the underlying model for analysis. The work done in (Gokhale & Trivedi, 2006) proposes a unifying framework for state-based models for architecture-based software reliability prediction. The models used are discrete time Markov chain (DTMC), or a continuous time Markov chain (CTMC). They discuss the input required and the estimate to be made from different artifacts. Palviainen, Evesti, and Ovaska (2011), address software reliability evaluation during the design and implementation phases. The authors contribute by integrating the component-level reliability evaluation activities and the system-level reliability prediction activity to support the incremental and iterative development. Also a tool chain was developed to support the usage of reliability evaluation approach.

Chong and Lee (2015) proposes an approach to represent an object-oriented software system using a weighted complex network in order to capture its structural characteristics, with respect to its maintainability and reliability analysis. The software architecture is transformed into a weighted complex network that assigns weights based on the complexity of relationships and classes from UML class diagrams calculated from CK metrics. Graph theory metrics (such as in-degree, out-degree, average weighted degree, average shortest path of nodes, average clustering coefficient, and betweenness centrality) are applied onto the transformed network to evaluate the software system for maintainability and reliability measures. Chun Shan et al. (2019) apply the concept of weighted complex network to study the structural features of the software, to predict its quality parameters such as reliability and security. The network is constructed from the UML diagrams of the source code. They use measures such as degree of the node, entropy measures, degree of inheritance, and the degree of ripple.

Ontology based software architecture knowledge representation are widely studied as a tool for architecture documentation, knowledge retrieval and analysis techniques. Graaf et al. (2014) discuss the techniques for constructing ontology for software architecture that suits the needs of different users. To empower ATAM, authors in (Erfanian & Aliee, 2008) propose Attribute-Based Architectural styles (ABAS) using ontology for reusability of architectural knowledge. Ovaska et al. (2010) proposes quality aware software architecting approach and a supporting tool chain that enables the systematic development of high quality software by merging benefits of knowledge modeling and management, and model driven architecture design enhanced with domain-specific quality attributes.

The analysis of software architecture can be broadly classified as qualitative and quantitative methods. Qualitative techniques make use of questionnaires, checklists and scenarios for evaluation; whereas the quantitative techniques rely on metrics, prototypes, simulations, etc. Scenario based methods and software metrics are popular among these evaluation methods. Some of these methods are SAAM, ATAM, CBAM, ALMA, and FAAM. The processes followed in these methods are detailed in (Dobrica, L., & Niemela, E., 2002; Zhu, Aurum, Gorton et al., 2005). Each of these methods assesses different quality factors including modifiability, extensibility, interoperability, etc. The key metrics/tools considered in these methods are scenarios, time, cost, various tables and figures. These methods rarely make use of mathematical models for quality evaluation. Each one has its own strengths and weaknesses. A general analysis of these models show that these require detailed knowledge of the underlying architecture, no clear metrics for quality prediction, consumes considerable efforts in carrying out the process by conducting meeting with various stakeholders, and preparation of certain artifacts that aid in the quality evaluation process.

Software Metrics are used to quantitatively measure these quality parameters and to assess the quality of the overall software system. Software Metric Suites provide various metrics that can be measured at different levels of the software such as design level, or code level for the quality assessment. There are three famous metric suites available in the literature for the Object Oriented Software Systems. They are the Chidamber and Kemerer (CK) metrics, Abreu's Metrics for Object-Oriented Design (MOOD), and Bansiya and Davis' Quality Metrics for Object-Oriented Design (QMOOD). These metrics are detailed in the literature in Chidamber & Kemerer, 1994; Abreu & Melo, 1996; and Bansiya & Davis, 2002. Olague et al., (2007) provide a validation of the three metrics suites in identifying the fault proneness of a class. They concluded that CK and QMOOD provide similar models in detecting the error-prone classes and MOOD metric suite is not good with such error predictors. The authors in (Radjenovic, Hericko, Torkar, & Zivkovi, 2013) studied the applicability of metrics to fault prediction based on context properties. They found that the CK metrics are popularly used in object oriented systems. These metrics perform better compared to the existing traditional and complexity measures. The three metric suites of CK, MOOD and Martin are compared for package level metrics such as size, complexity and cohesion by Elish, Al-Yafei, and Al-Mulhem (2011). In their work, the authors concluded Martin suite performs better for pre-release and post-release faults. Misra et al. (2018) provides a suite of cognitive complexity metrics for object orientation systems. Using these, an insight on the maintainability and reliability can be arrived. The proposal is validate both theoretically and empirically.

The summary of the key processes and the concepts involved in architectural quality analysis is given in Table 2. Even though the evaluation process consumes considerable efforts, the benefits are worth noting. They are listed below:

- Prioritized Statement of conflicting Quality Attribute Requirements – the evaluation process puts stakeholders at various levels in one room. This help the analysts and the developers to resolve the conflicts and ambiguity and arriving at a prioritized set of requirements.

- Mapping of Approaches to Quality Attributes – a detailed understanding of the quality requirements assist the developers to select the best approaches to achieve the desired quality.
- Risks and Non-risks – risk management is a crucial activity in any software development. Risks are highly uncertain and the architecture evaluation process helps to reduce project risks to certain extent.
- Puts Stakeholders in the Same Room – it is highly recommended to communicate and resolve the conflicting requirements and the open discussion of the requirements help to understand the system better which facilitates the success of the project according to the market demands and customer needs.
- Improves the Quality of Architectural Documentation – the evaluation process is directly involved in improving the quality of the architecture by selecting more appropriate design choices.
- Uncovers Opportunities for Cross-Project Reuse – this is possible due to the communication of experts in different areas and knowledge on multiple projects facilitates reuse across organizational level.
- Results in Improved Architecture Practices – the good and bad practices are shared across projects and helps in the maturity level of the organization.

THE SOURCE CODE QUALITY

During the development phase, the source code of the product is written from the base lined design documents. The implementation of the software follows an iterative method in Agile development methodology. This section presents the results from the literature for the search of desired characteristics to be possessed by the source code. These characteristics build a quality product that is reliable, secure, and maintainable and other such quality attributes discussed in the earlier sections. The software quality models insist on the development of reliable and robust software products. Software Reliability refers to the probability of failure-free operation of the software for a specified period of time under specified environment. Fault prevention, fault removal, fault tolerances are three methods to achieve reliable software. The current practices of software reliability measurement can be divided into four categories. They are Product metrics, Project management metrics, Process metrics, Fault and failure metrics. Software Reliability Models are used for the software reliability analysis. The authors in (Yacoub, Cukic, & Ammar, 2004) propose a scenario based reliability analysis for component-based software. A Component-Dependency Graph is constructed and the reliability algorithm is run to predict the variations and uncertainties in individual components.

Table 2. Highlights of Architectural Design Study

Architectural Quality Processes	
Literature Reference	Discussion
Modeling Choices	
Zhou et al. (2009) Zhang, and Yan (2011)	Fuzzy UML
Wang, Pan, and Chen (2006) Sharma and Trivedi (2006) Gokhale and Trivedi (2006)	DTMC/CTMC
Chong and Lee (2015) Chun Shan et al. (2019)	Complex Networks
Graaf et al. (2014) Erfanian and Aliee (2008)	Ontology
Quality Attributes	
Wang, Pan, and Chen (2006) Sharma and Trivedi (2006) Palviainen, Evesti, and Ovaska (2011) Chong and Lee (2015)	Reliability
Chong and Lee (2015)	Maintainability
Sharma and Trivedi (2006) Chun Shan et al. (2019)	Security
Metrics Suites	
Chidamber and Kemerer (1994) Olague et al., (2007) Radjenovic, Hericko, Torkar, and Zivkovi (2013)	CK metrics
Abreu and Melo (1996) Olague et al. (2007)	MOOD
Bansiya and Davis (2002) Olague et al. (2007)	QMOOD

S. Martínez-Fernández et al. (2019) propose a software analysis tool, which integrates the quality models that improves the quality in addition to static code analysis. The deployment of the tool is done by four companies and the paper discusses the challenges and the lessons in developing such as code quality improvement tool. M Azeem Akbar et al. (2017) propose a new AZ-Model for Software Development Life Cycle. This model has three phases, namely the customer involvement phase, development phase and the release phase. Time boxing and strong project management are introduced as key concepts in the model. A survey was conducted for the proposed model to identify its suitability and the results reveal the model is effective.

Robustness refers to the ability of the software to cope with errors that may occur during the execution and continue its operation. Resiliency refers to the capability of the software to recover from such erroneous conditions while continuing to be functional. Fault injection is a testing method widely used to test the robustness and resiliency of the software, which involves introducing faults to test the execution path of the source code. It is an important stress testing mechanism in building a robust software product. Winter, Sarbu, Suri, and Murphy (2011), uses Software-implemented fault injection (SWIFI) approach for evaluating the robustness of software components. The authors in (Maxion & Olszewski, 1998) studied the improvement of robustness for exception failures though dependability cases. These dependability cases use the structural characteristics of the software components in improving the error handling mechanism. Shahrokni and Feldt (2013) performed a systematic review on software robustness on Commercial Off The Shelf (COTS) products and concluded that more robustness research is required on real world projects and must be insisted during requirements engineering itself. In (Huang, Peled, Schewe, & Wang, 2016), a game theoretic approach is proposed in order to validate the resilience of a software system against k dense errors. The authors have designed a two-player concurrent game model with the application of alternating-time μ-calculus (AMC) with an extension. The analysis has been modeled as a model checking problem for the software to be resilient to utmost k dense errors. Camara et al., (2017) propose a method for validating resilience in self-adaptive systems based on probabilistic model checking. Raja and Tretter (2012) define and validate a measure of project viability, which has the dimensions of vigor, resilience, and organization. They define a viability index combining the three dimensions and demonstrate this index is robust in measuring the project survivability.

In the more recent software trends, in addition to being robust and resilient, the software is required to be Antifragile. Antifragility is the negative of fragility. An antifragile system gets better by exposure to disorder, shock or uncertainties. An antifragile system is able to evolve its identity by learning from the disorder and by improving itself. Antifragility is the concept developed by Professor Nassim Nicolas Taleb in 2012 (Taleb, 2012). This concept has been applied in various fields such as biology, physics, and Computer science. "Antifragile Software Manifesto" (Russoa & Ciancarinia, 2016) is a proposal, which is still in the phases of infantry, invites proposals from the research community to incorporate antifragility in the system design process. It lists various principles that need to be practiced to build systems that improve from the input from the environment and making it antifragile. Taleb in his book (Taleb, 2012) describes the concepts of antifragility, its properties, the non-predictive view of the world and various mathematical techniques to detect antifragility. Anti-Fragility can also be proposed as an Anti-Ageing solution to software systems. Fragile, Robust and Antifragile are defined as a triad in explaining the desirable properties of software. A fragile is one which is easily breakable to any disturbance. A robust system resists and withstands such shocks to some extent, but it remains the same. Antifragility is beyond resilience or robustness.

There are only a few literatures that describe the concepts of antifragility and building the same in the software development processes. Attila and Svetinovic (2013) describe the process of identifying fragile components from the requirements specification. A case study of crowdsourcing is taken and its requirements specification is analyzed for five signs of fragility. Finally eight fragility-related requirements are arrived for the chosen case study. This work identifies only the requirements that cause the software system to be fragile. But, no measures are posed to build antifragility into the software. Thus there is a need for a method to develop an antifragile system with the existing framework of Object Oriented System development. The author in (Russoa & Ciancarinia, 2017) discusses the effectiveness of antifragile software compared to traditional approaches. Here, antifragility in software architecture is suggested by using fine grained architectures. Antifragility mainly addresses the protection of the software systems from the Black Swans. Black swam theory is a metaphor that describes an event that comes as a surprise. These events have a major impact on the system and often hard to predict (Taleb, 2008). An antifragile system has characteristics of being immune against these types of outliers.

SOFTWARE REFACTORING FOR QUALITY IMPROVEMENT

Software evolves during its lifetime and the major cause for the evolution is the change in the operating environment or the functionality upgrade required due to advancements in hardware and other technologies. This change impacts the reliability and the flexibility of the software system. The frequency of this software evolution is more in the current software trends. Code Refactoring is an important maintenance activity of any software that restorers the quality level of the software to acceptable limit.

Refactoring, as defined by Martin Fowler and kent Beck (Fowler at al., 1999) is:

"A change made to the internal structure of software to make it easier to understand and cheaper to modify without changing its observable behavior. It is a disciplined way to clean up code that minimizes the chances of introducing bugs."

Software refactoring aims to improve the internal structure of the source code without affecting its external behavior and is carried out considering the quality goals on the priority list during the maintenance of any software. Refactoring is concerned with the improvement in the non-functional attributes of software, making the code readable, less complex and improving its maintainability and extensibility.

Refactoring and quality attributes go hand-in-hand, meaning that the effectiveness of refactoring is quantified using some selected and prioritized quality attributes. Quality factors are the indicators of the goodness of a design or code of a software product. Famous well established quality factors are Abstraction, Inheritance, Coupling and Cohesion. The Technical Debt (TD) is another quality factor that is prevalent in the recent times in the software quality analysis. The description of these quality factors are given in Table 2.

TD is a metaphor that denotes the efforts that are required to perform the pending changes that need to be done in the software (Kruchten, Nord, Ozkaya, & Visser, 2012). These pending changes exist as the result of choosing an easy solution instead of a more appropriate one, which would rather take more time to implement. This decision may be made due to a number of factors such as meeting of deadline, insufficient requirements, lack of technical knowledge, etc. This incurred TD has to be repaid in later point of time with interest. Hence, with time, it is difficult to add or modify functionalities due to the structure of the software becoming cumbersome. The technical debt is repaid by using Software Refactoring and is an important, inevitable and effective technique in ensuring the quality of the software. The authors in (Behutiye, Rodríguez, Oivo, & Tosun, 2017), discusses the literature on analyzing the TD in agile development environment. It discusses the strategies for management of TD from the architectural perspective. Ramasubbu and Kermerer (2017) in their work discuss a framework for management of Technical Debt in the Software quality management processes. The framework is proposed as a three step process, which consists of tracking the TD, performing a cost-benefit analysis for identifying the implications of the TD, and controlling the TD by applying changes to the architectural and the module levels. The framework is applied to three real time projects in different organizations and the outcome is validated. By applying the

Table 3. Quality Factors for Refactoring

Quality Parameters	Description
Abstraction	A measure that denotes how easy the system can be extended by suppressing more complex details in the levels below.
Inheritance	A measure of structural reuse that enables the new objects to inherit the properties of existing objects.
Coupling	A measure of interdependence between software modules and the strength of relationship between the classes.
Cohesion	A measure of strength of relationship between the elements inside a module in which they belong
Technical Debt	A metaphor that represents the extra development efforts that are required to change the code that has been implemented in easy way in short run instead of applying the best solution. TD paid at a later point incurs interest.

proposal, the organizations were able to achieve economic gains. In (MacCormack & Daniel, 2016), the authors address the concept of architectural debts, by analyzing the relationship between the architecture and the maintenance costs by assessing the coupling among different components of the system.

Vassallo et al. (2019) conducted an exploration of 200 open source software for the process of refactoring. They concluded that the source code is refactored less frequently to improve the understanding of the code. The process of refactoring is done on the stable version of the software by the owners of the code. Ying et al. (2017), propose a refactoring algorithm that refactors at the system level based on high cohesion and low coupling. The algorithm merges and splits related classes and regroups the entities. The refactoring suggestions are provided based on the benefits the can bring to the code and the comparative results show better performance. An empirical evaluation of the process of refactoring on internal and external quality attributes was done by Dallal and Abdin (2017). The results show that different refactoring activities have negative impact on other quality parameter. Hence, they concluded that refactoring always do not better result with respect to the overall quality of the system.

Optimization problems are class of decision problems where, there exists a set of feasible solution out of which a favorable solution, called the optimal solution is to be identified. This optimal solution is arrived at by maximizing or minimizing certain criteria, which is termed as the objective function. There can be multiple criteria with a combination of maximization or minimization functions. These classes of problems are termed as Multi-Objective optimization problems. Heuristic algorithms are designed to solve a problem more efficiently than the traditional methods, where approximate solutions are sufficient to yield better results compared to the exact solutions, which are otherwise computationally expensive. In Search-Based Software Engineering (SBSE), majority of the problems are solved preferably with meta-heuristics, since deterministic methods are not suitable to these kinds of real world problems. These meta-heuristics generate a set of candidate solutions and evaluate against the given criteria and return the optimal solution when the stopping criterion is reached. Hill climbing, Simulated Annealing, population based techniques such as Evolutionary Algorithms (EA) and Genetic Algorithms (GA) are the popular of these methods. Many bio-inspired algorithms are also popular like Particle Swarm Optimization (PSO), Artificial Bee Colony (ABC), Ant Colony Optimization (ACO) to name a few. The problem of software refactoring can be formulated as Multi-Objective Optimization problem. The use of optimization techniques is proved to yield better results with respect to various quality constraints called the fitness functions. There can be multiple such quality constraints in which the applied algorithm is expected to produce better results. While formulating such a problem, the search space consists of the refactoring locations of the software code, upon which the optimization techniques are applied to arrive at a strategy for refactoring for improving multiple quality constraints.

Over the past few years, the application of Search Based Software Engineering in the problem of Software Refactoring has produced many notable research works. One of which is the work done my Mohan et al. (2016), where the authors use a combination of automated refactoring tools, metaheuristic techniques and software metrics to manage the technical debt. Here, multiple quality attributes are used to access the effectiveness of their proposed method. O'Keeffe and O'Cinnéide (2008a) discusses about the use of automated software refactoring in order to reduce the maintenance cost. A tool CODe-Imp has been developed and the results are studied by using QMOOD metrics applied for sample Java projects. Simulated annealing searches were found to be effective in the experiment. In (M. O'Keeffe & O'Cinnéide, 2008b), the authors applied different techniques for Search-Based Software Engineering such as, simulated annealing, genetic algorithms and multiple ascent hill-climbing. The tool CODe-Imp has been employed to study the quality model of the refactorings applied on five input programs. They have concluded that multiple-ascent hill climbing outperform other compared algorithms. Koc et al. (2012), studied the performance of automated refactoring modelled as combinatorial optimization problem. Here, 20 different refactoring actions are applied and the performance is studied by combination of 24 object-oriented software metrics. A tool called A-CMA was developed that applies the refactoring actions on the sample Java programs input and comparing the refactoring with random, steepest descent, multiple first descent, multiple steepest descent, simulated annealing and artificial bee colony algorithms.

In the paper (Ghannem, El Boussaidi, & Kessentini, 2014), the authors consider the refactoring mechanism as a combinatorial optimization problem and refactor from examples. The models are evaluated based on a set of structural metrics. Here, genetic algorithm is applied on open source projects and the effectiveness of the approach is evaluated based on precision and recall metrics. In (Mkaouer et al., 2015a), the authors formulated the problem of software refactoring as a multiple objective problem and applied NSGA-III algorithm with eight distinct objectives. They studied the findings comparing to several other many-objective techniques and used one industrial project and seven open source systems. To remove code-smells, in (Ouni, Kessentini, Bechikh, & Sahraoui, 2015), refactoring operations are used to improve the design of the software by prioritizing the refactoring options. A chemical reaction optimization is used which is shown to provide better results compared to other existing techniques.

Mkaouer et al. (2015b) propose a many-objective NSGA-III algorithm to improve the automation of software re-modularization. The algorithm aims at finding the optimal re-modularization solutions considering multiple objectives such as improving

Table 4. Highlights of Source Code Quality Improvement Study

Source code Quality Processes	
Literature Reference	**Discussion**
Desired Source Code Property	
Yacoub, Cukic, and Ammar (2004)	Reliability
Winter, Sarbu, Suri, and Murphy (2011) Maxion and Olszewski (1998) Shahrokni and Feldt (2013)	Robustness
Huang, Peled, Schewe, and Wang (2016) Camara et al. (2017) Raja and Tretter (2012)	Resilience
Taleb (2012) Russoa and Ciancarinia (2016) Russoa and Ciancarinia (2017)	Antifragility
Quality Attributes & Refactoring	
Ying et al. (2017)	Coupling & Cohesion
Kruchten, Nord, Ozkaya, and Visser (2012) Behutiye, Rodríguez, Oivo, and Tosun (2017) Ramasubbu and Kermerer (2017) Mohan et al. (2016)	Technical Debt
Meta-heuristics & Refactoring	
Mohan et al. (2016)	A-CMA tool
O'Keeffe and O'Cinnéide (2008a)	CODe-Imp tool
M. O'Keeffe and O'Cinnéide (2008b)	Simulated Annealing
Koc et al. (2012)	Artificial Bee Colony
Ghannem, El Boussaidi, and Kessentini (2014)	Genetic Algorithm
Mkaouer et al. (2015a) Mkaouer et al. (2015b)	NSGA-III
Ouni, Kessentini, Bechikh, and Sahraoui (2015)	Chemical reaction optimization

the structure of packages, minimizing the number of changes, preserving semantics coherence, and the reuse of the history of changes. The approach has been evaluated using four different open-source systems and one automotive industry project and the results are validated using quantitative and qualitative methods. Wang, Pan, Jiang, and Yuan (2015) performed a study that uses a bipartite network to represent classes and a new bipartite modularity metric is introduced to quantify the modularity of a software system. The authors proposed an approach for identifying the methods that should be moved between classes. In (Mkaouer et al., 2016), the authors applied NSGA-II for the software refactoring problem for trade-off between three objectives to maximize, namely the quality improvements, severity and importance of refactoring opportunities. The authors in (Ouni et al., 2016), propose a multi-objective search-based approach for automating the refactoring recommendation by optimizing multiple criteria such as minimizing the number of design defects, minimizing code changes required, preserving design semantics, maximizing the consistency with the previously code changes. An industrial validation of the technique has been performed and arrived at successful results. Varghese, Raimond and Lovesum (2019) proposed an approach for software re-modularization using an extended Ant Colony Optimization technique for easily maintenance and quality improvement of the system. The performance of their proposed method is validated using Turbo Modularization Quality parameter, applied to similar algorithms such as Genetic Algorithm, Hill Climbing and Interactive Genetic Algorithms. The discussion on the approaches on improving source code quality by developmental requirements and the refactoring process is given in Table 4.

CONCLUSION

The objective of this study is to gather the quality enhancement techniques available for the architecture design and the desirable characteristics of source code of the software product. These two artifacts are chosen since these are the fundamental outputs that decide the success of the project. All other phases and processes are involved in quality improvisation of these two artifacts including the testing phase. A detailed study on the architectural level quality analysis is done. From the study it is noted that the architectural quality analysis should start from the initial design phases itself to predict the quality factors and take necessary actions for improvising the same. Depending on the nature of the product, a suitable architectural model can be selected and the quality analysis can be initiated. Scenario based architectural analysis techniques are popular. But these techniques require experienced analysts and various stakeholders to be present during the quality analysis process. These techniques suffer from the drawbacks in terms of time and expertise. Hence, a more realistic, precise, automated technique for architectural quality analysis needs to be developed.

From the development perspective, the source code is desired to possess the properties of reliability, robustness, and resilience. Anti-fragility is defined beyond robustness and resiliency. Changes to the process of software development are invited to take the source to the next step of being antifragile. Self-adaptive and self-repairing systems are more desirable in the current software trends. Hence, more research is required in these areas of software development. Quality improvement cannot be completed without the process of Software Refactoring. Irrespective of the measures taken during the development of software in earlier phases, like the analysis, design, development and testing, there always exists a scope for quality improvement during maintenance. Technical debt is an important factor that needs to be maintained low and refactoring process is effective in achieving this task. Other quality factors such as abstraction, inheritance, and coupling can be used as good indicators to achieve improvement in quality during refactoring. Search-based techniques are applied in software refactoring to arrive at an optimal strategy for source code refactoring. Other innovative and automated techniques can be explored to provide better and faster improvement in quality during refactoring. Hence, this study concludes there are many future research directions are available in quality improvement that are worth exploring.

REFERENCES

Abreu, F. B., & Melo, W. (1996). Evaluating the Impact of Object Oriented Design on Software Quality. *Proc. Third Int'l Software Metrics Symp.*, 90-99. 10.1109/METRIC.1996.492446

Akbar, M. A. (2017). Improving the quality of software development process by introducing a new methodology - AZ-Model. *IEEE Access: Practical Innovations, Open Solutions*. doi:10.1109/ACCESS.2017.2787981

Al-Badareen, A. B., Selamat, M. H., Jabar, M. A., Din, J., & Turaev, S. (2011). Software Quality Models: A Comparative Study. ICSECS 2011, 179, 46–55.

Attila, P. T., & Svetinovic, D. (2013). Identifying Signs of Systems Fragility: A Crowdsourcing Requirements Case Study. *Proceedings of the IEEE IEEM*.

Bansiya, J., & Davis, C. (2002). A Hierarchical Model for Object Oriented Design Quality Assessment. *IEEE Transactions on Software Engineering*, 28(1), 4-17.

Bass, L., Clements, P., & Kazman, R. (2013). *Software Architecture in Practice. SEI Series in Software Engineering* (3rd ed.). Pearson Education, Inc.

Behutiye, W., Rodríguez, P., Oivo, M., & Tosun, A. (2017). Analyzing the concept of technical debt in the context of agile software development: A systematic literature review. *Information and Software Technology*, 82, 139–158. doi:10.1016/j.infsof.2016.10.004

Camara, J., Lemos, R., Laranjeiro, R., Ventura, R., & Vieira, M. (2017). Robustness-Driven Resilience Evaluation of Self-Adaptive Software Systems. *IEEE Transactions on Dependable and Secure Computing*, 14–1.

Chidamber, S., & Kemerer, C. (1994). A metrics suite for object oriented design. *IEEE Transactions on Software Engineering, 20*(6), 476–493. doi:10.1109/32.295895

Chong, C. Y., & Lee, S. P. (2015). Analyzing maintainability and reliability of object-oriented software using weighted complex network. *The Journal of Systems and Software, Elsevier, 110*, 28–53. doi:10.1016/j.jss.2015.08.014

Dallal, J. A., & Abdin, A. (2017). Empirical Evaluation of the Impact of Object-Oriented Code Refactoring on Quality Attributes: A Systematic Literature Review. *IEEE Transactions on Software Engineering.* doi:10.1109/TSE.2017.2658573

Das, S., Dewanji, A., & Chakraborty, A. (2016). Software Reliability Modeling With Periodic Debugging Schedule. *IEEE Transactions on Reliability, 65*(3), 1449–1456. doi:10.1109/TR.2016.2570572

Dobrica, L., & Niemela, E. (2002). A survey on software architecture analysis methods. *IEEE Transactions on Software Engineering, 28*(7), 638-653.

Elish, M. O., Al-Yafei, A. H., & Al-Mulhem, M. (2011). Empirical comparison of three metrics suites for fault prediction in packages of object-oriented systems: A case study of Eclipse. *Advances in Engineering Software, 42*(10), 852–859. doi:10.1016/j.advengsoft.2011.06.001

Erfanian, A., & Aliee, F. S. (2008). *An Ontology-Driven Software Architecture Evaluation Method. SHARK'08.* Leipzig, Germany: ACM.

Fernández, M. S. (2019). Continuously Assessing and Improving Software Quality With Software Analytics Tools: A Case Study. *IEEE Access: Practical Innovations, Open Solutions, 7.*

Fowler, M., Beck, K., Brant, J., Opdyke, W., & Roberts, D. (1999). *Refactoring: Improving the Design of Existing Code.* Addison-Wesley Professional.

Ghannem, A., El Boussaidi, G., & Kessentini, M. (2014). Model refactoring using examples: a search-based approach. *J. Softw. Evolution. Process, 26*(7), 692–713.

Gokhale, S. S., & Trivedi, K. S. (2006). Analytical Models for Architecture-Based Software Reliability Prediction: A Unification Framework. *IEEE Transactions on Reliability*, 55–4.

Graaf, K. A., Liang, P., Tang, A., Hage, W. R. V., & Vliet, H. V. (2014). An exploratory study on ontology engineering for software architecture documentation. *Computers in Industry, 65*(7), 1053-1064.

Huang, C. H., Peled, D. A., Schewe, S., & Wang, F. (2016). A Game-Theoretic Foundation for the Maximum Software Resilience against Dense Errors. *IEEE Transactions on Software Engineering*, 42–47.

IEEE. (1991). *IEEE Std 610.12-1990 – IEEE Standard Glossary of Software Engineering Terminology*. New York: IEEE Software Engineering Standards Collection.

ISO/IEC. (2011). *ISO/IEC 25010:2011: Systems and software engineering - Systems and software Quality Requirements and Evaluation (SQuaRE) - System and software quality models*. International Organization for Standardization.

ISO/IEC TR 9126-2. (2003). *Software Engineering - Product Quality - Part 2: External Metrics*. International Organization for Standardization.

Koc, E., Ersoy, N., Andac, A., Camlidere, Z. S., Cereci, I., & Kilic, H. (2012). An empirical study about search-based refactoring using alternative multiple and population-based search techniques. In E. Gelenbe, R. Lent, & G. Sakellari (Eds.), *Comput. Inf. Sci. II* (pp. 59–66). London: Springer.

Kruchten, P., Nord, R. L., Ozkaya, I., & Visser, J. (2012). Technical Debt in Software Development: from Metaphor to Theory. *ACM SIGSOFT Software Engineering Notes*, *37*(5), 36.

Ma, Z. M., Zhang, F., & Yan, L. (2011). Fuzzy information modeling in UML class diagram and relational database models. *Applied Soft Computing, Elsevier*, *11*(6), 4236–4245. doi:10.1016/j.asoc.2011.03.020

MacCormack, A., & Daniel, J. S. (2016). Technical debt and system architecture: The impact of coupling on defect-related activity. *Journal of Systems and Software*, *120*, 170–182. doi:10.1016/j.jss.2016.06.007

Maxion, R. A., & Olszewski, R. T. (1998). Improving Software Robustness with Dependability Cases. In *The Twenty-Eighth International Symposium on Fault-Tolerant Computing*. IEEE Computer Society Press. 10.1109/FTCS.1998.689485

Miguel, P. J., Mauricio, D., & Rodríguez, G. (2014). A Review of Software Quality Models for the Evaluation of Software Products. *International Journal of Software Engineering and Its Applications*, *5-6*, 31. doi:10.5121/ijsea.2014.5603

Misra, S., Adewumi, A., Fernandez, L. S., & Damasevicius, R. (2018). A Suite of Object Oriented Cognitive Complexity Metrics. *IEEE Access: Practical Innovations, Open Solutions*, *6*, 8782–8796. doi:10.1109/ACCESS.2018.2791344

Mkaouer, M. W., Kessentini, M., Bechikh, S., O'Cinnéide, M., & Deb, K. (2015a). On the use of many quality attributes for software refactoring: A many-objective search-based software engineering approach. *Empirical Software Engineering*, 1–43.

Mkaouer, M. W., Kessentini, M., O'Cinnéide, M., Hayash, S., & Deb, K. (2016). A robust multi-objective approach to balance severity and importance of refactoring opportunities. *Empirical Software Engineering*, 1–43.

Mkaouer, W., Kessentini, M., Kontchou, P., Deb, K., Bechikh, S., & Ouni, A. (2015b). Many-Objective Software Remodularization Using NSGA-III. *Trans. Softw. Eng. Methodol.*, *24*(3), 1–45.

Mohan, M. (2016). Technical debt reduction using search based automated refactoring. *The Journal of Systems and Software*. Doi:10.1016/j.jss.2016.05.019

National Institute of Standards and Technology. (2002). *The Economic Impacts of Inadequate Infrastructure for Software Testing*. Author.

O'Keeffe, M., & O'Cinnéide, M. (2008a). Search-based refactoring for software maintenance. *J. Syst. Softw.*, *81*(4), 502–516.

O'Keeffe, M. & O'Cinnéide, M. (2008b). Search-based refactoring: an empirical study. *J. Softw. Maint. Evolut.: Res. Pract.*, *20*(5), 345–364.

Olague, H. M., Etzkorn, L. H., Gholston, S., & Quattlebaum, S. (2007). Empirical Validation of Three Software Metrics Suites to Predict Fault-Proneness of Object-Oriented Classes Developed Using Highly Iterative or Agile Software Development Processes. *IEEE Transactions on Software Engineering*, *33*(6), 402 – 419.

Ouni, A., Kessentini, M., Bechikh, S., & Sahraoui, H. (2015). Prioritizing code-smells correction tasks using chemical reaction optimization. *Softw. Qual. J.*, *23*(2), 323–361.

Ouni, A., Kessentini, M., Sahraoui, H., Inoue, K., & Deb, K. (2016). Multi-criteria code refactoring using search-based software engineering: An industrial case study. *ACM Trans. Softw. Eng. Methodol.*, *25*(3), 1–53.

Ovaska, E., Evesti, A., Henttonen, K., Palviainen, M., & Aho, P. (2010). Knowledge based quality-driven architecture design and evaluation. *Information and Software Technology*, *52*(6), 577-601.

Palviainen, M., Evesti, A., & Ovaska, E. (2011). The reliability estimation, prediction and measuring of component-based software. *The Journal of Systems and Software, Elsevier*, *84*(6), 1054–1070. doi:10.1016/j.jss.2011.01.048

Radjenovic, D., Hericko, M., Torkar, R., & Zivkovi, A. (2013). Software Fault Prediction Metrics: A Systematic Literature Review. *Information and Software Technology, 55*(8), 1397–1418. doi:10.1016/j.infsof.2013.02.009

Raja, U., & Tretter, M. J. (2012). Defining and Evaluating a Measure of Open Source Project Survivability. *IEEE Transactions on Software Engineering*, 38–1.

Ramasubbu, N., & Kemerer, C. F. (2017). *Integrating Technical Debt Management and Software Quality Management Processes: A Normative Framework and Field Tests. IEEE Transactions on Software Engineering.* doi:10.1109/TSE.2017.2774832

Russoa, D., & Ciancarinia, P. (2016). A Proposal for an Antifragile Software Manifesto. *Procedia Computer Science, 83*, 982–987. doi:10.1016/j.procs.2016.04.196

Russoa, D., & Ciancarinia, P. (2017). Towards Antifragile Software Architectures. *4th International Workshop on Computational Antifragility and Antifragile Engineering, ANTIFRAGILE 2017.*

Shahrokni, A., & Feldt, R. (2013). A systematic review of software robustness. *Information and Software Technology, 55*(1), 1–17. doi:10.1016/j.infsof.2012.06.002

Shan, C., Mei, S., Hu, C., Liu, L., & Mao, L. (2019). Software structure characteristic measurement method based on weighted network. *Computer Networks, 152*, 178–185. doi:10.1016/j.comnet.2019.01.037

Sharma, V.S., & Trivedi, K. S. (2006). Quantifying software performance, reliability and security: An architecture-based approach. *The Journal of Systems and Software, Elsevier.*

Taleb, N. N. (2008). *The black swan: the impact of the highly improbable* (2nd ed.). London: Penguin.

Taleb, N. N. (2012). *Antifragile: Things That Gain From Disorder* (1st ed.). New York: Random House, Inc.

Varghese, B. G. R., Raimond, K., & Lovesum, J. (2019). A Novel Approach for Automatic Remodularization of Software Systems using Extended Ant Colony Optimization Algorithm. *Information and Software Technology, 114*, 107–120. doi:10.1016/j.infsof.2019.06.002

Vassallo, C., Grano, G., Palomba, F., Gall, H. C., & Bacchelli, A. (2019). A large-scale empirical exploration on refactoring activities in open source software projects. *Science of Computer Programming, 180*, 1–15. doi:10.1016/j.scico.2019.05.002

Wang, M., Pan, W., Jiang, B., & Yuan, C. (2015). CLEAR: class level soft- ware refactoring using evolutionary algorithms. *J. Intell. Syst.*, *24*(1), 85–97.

Wang, W. L., Pan, D., & Chen, M. H. (2006). Architecture-based software reliability modeling. *Journal of Systems and Software*, *79*(1), 132–146. doi:10.1016/j.jss.2005.09.004

Winter, S., Sarbu, C., Suri, N., & Murphy, B. (2011). The impact of fault models on software robustness evaluations. *Proc. Intl. Conf. on Software Engineering*, 51–60. 10.1145/1985793.1985801

Yacoub, S., Cukic, B., & Ammar, H. H. (2004). A Scenario-Based Reliability Analysis Approach for Component-Based Software. *IEEE Transactions on Reliability*, 53–54.

Ying, W., Hai, Y., Zhi-Liang, Z., Wei, Z., & Yu-Li, Z. (2017). Automatic Software Refactoring via Weighted Clustering in Method-level Networks. *IEEE Transactions on Software Engineering*. doi:10.1109/TSE.2017.2679752

Zhou, B., Lu, J., Wang, Z., Zhang, Y., & Miao, Z. (2009). Formalizing Fuzzy UML Class Diagrams with Fuzzy Description Logics. *Third International Symposium on Intelligent Information Technology Application*. 10.1109/IITA.2009.97

Zhu, L., Aurum, A., Gorton, I., & Jeffery, R. (2005). Tradeoff and Sensitivity Analysis in Software Architecture Evaluation Using Analytic Hierarchy Process. *Software Quality Journal*, *13*(4), 357–375. doi:10.100711219-005-4251-0

ADDITIONAL READING

Allspaw, J. (2012). Fault injection in production. *Communications of the ACM*, *55*(10), 48–52. doi:10.1145/2347736.2347751

Basiri, A., Behnam, N., Rooij, D., Hochstein, L., Kosewski, L., Reynolds, J., & Rosenthal, C. (2016). Chaos engineering. *IEEE Computer*, *33*(3), 35–41.

Bavota, G. (2010). Playing with Refactoring: Identifying Extract Class Opportunities through Game Theory. *26th IEEE International Conference on Software Maintenance*. 10.1109/ICSM.2010.5609739

Cartwright, M., & Shepperd, M. (2000). An Empirical Investigation of an Object-Oriented Software System. *IEEE Transactions on Software Engineering*, 26–28.

Kazman, R., Bass, L., Klein, M., Lattanze, T., & Northrop, L. (2005). A Basis for Analyzing Software Architecture Analysis Methods. *Software Quality Journal*, *13*(4), 329–355. doi:10.100711219-005-4250-1

Koru, A. G., Zhang, D., El Emam, K., & Liu, H. (2009). An Investigation into the Functional Form of the Size-Defect Relationship for Software Modules. *IEEE Transactions on Software Engineering*, 35 - 2, pp. 293-304.

Kumar, K., & Prabhakar, T. V. (2009). Quality Attribute Game: A Game Theory Based Technique for Software Architecture Design. *Proceeding of the 2nd annual conference on India software engineering conference, ACM*, pp. 133–134: Pune, India.

Monperrus, M. (2017). Principles of Antifragile Software. Programming '17 ACM: Brussels, Belgium.

Pan, W. (2011). Applying Complex Network Theory to Software Structure Analysis. *International Journal of Computer, Electrical, Automation, Control and Information Engineering*, 5 - 12.

Yadav, H. B., & Yadav, D. K. (2015). A fuzzy logic based approach for phase-wise software defects prediction using software metrics. *Information and Software Technology*, *63*, 44–57. doi:10.1016/j.infsof.2015.03.001

KEY TERMS AND DEFINITIONS

Code Smells: The locations in source code where modifications can be made to improve the overall quality. These locations need not contain a bug but, improvement may prevent the bug in near future.

Fault Injection: It is a testing mechanism in which a fault is deliberated introduced in order to test the error handling functionality of the software to ensure its robustness.

Multi-Objective Optimization: Optimization problems arrive at a solution that best satisfies a goal. Multiple such goals need to be simultaneously satisfied for the class of Multi-Objective Optimization problems.

Non-Functional Requirement: The quality requirements that needs to be incorporated in order to achieve customer satisfaction. They are usually not specified as a part of requirements specification, but are essential for success of project.

Scenario-Based Evaluation: A method of assessment, where the software components are checked against a sequence of operation of the functional requirements.

Software Ageing: The degradation in the performance or failure of operation of the software due to continuously running and depleting the operating system resources. Software Rejuvenation is a proactive method proposed as a solution for ageing software.

Software Structural Characteristics: Structural characteristics represent the blue print of software components and their relationships and hierarchy to satisfy the design goals. The position of critical components and their connection are important in achieving the quality requirements.

Chapter 8
An Analysis of UI/UX Designing With Software Prototyping Tools

Shruti Gupta
Amity University, Delhi, India

ABSTRACT

In an age where everyone is carrying a smart phone, it is of utmost importance to make efficient use of the upcoming technologies. This indicates the rise in number of applications being created for mobile devices. As a result, mobile user interface designing has become a significant part of application designing. There has been an increasing number of devices today providing powerful graphics capabilities helping users to deal with huge amount of information. However, the prototyping tools currently being used in the industry are lacking features and are not addressing some of the prime issues like user friendliness, functionalities, representation, and enforcement. This chapter presents a tool based on an analysis of different popular prototyping tools in the industry which will overcome some or all of the major issues faced by application designers. The authors describe the prototyping tool's concept, design, features, as well as how it is suitable for making great user interfaces helping application designers to design exactly what they want.

INTRODUCTION

User interface designing focuses on firstly identifying the needs of the users and then creating an interface with functionalities which implements these user needs ensuring ease of access (Oppermann, 2002; Sharp, 2003; Wood, 1997). Thus, we see that mobile interaction design is a challenging procedure as the success or

DOI: 10.4018/978-1-5225-9659-2.ch008

failure of any application hinges on its ease of accessibility and understand ability (Myers, Hudson, & Pausch, 2000; Hix & Hartson, 1993). Due to cultural and literary differences, the usage of application varies and depends on demographics (Marcus & Gould, 2000). This clearly indicates the need of creating a prototype of software's or applications which will address the above issues. So what purpose do the prototypes have?

A prototype is created or developed to improve the efficiency of critical software developmental processes of planning and execution (Isreal & Lee, 2001). Pedro Szekely says that in order to develop complex applications, prototyping is an important stage which involves building a small scale version to reduce cost and risks involved (Szekely, 1994). It consists of some or all features of the software. The benefits from early prototyping are immense (Snyder, 2003). As said by Sidney L. Smith and Jane N. Mosier that designing of interfaces are time-consuming and costly but are very critical for the performance of the application (Smith & Mosier, 1986). The users can then use the prototype model of the software and give their feedback. The developers will gain a better understanding of what the requirements of the end users are and also if any modifications are needed (Hackos & Redish, 1998). This establishes good relations between users and developers which is ideal for any software project (Baumer, Bischofberger, Lichter & Zullighoven, 1996; Floyd, 1984).

Some designers in the beginning often create rough sketches of the screen layouts. Initially major design issues should be addressed rather than focussing on design details like color and alignment (Landay & Meyers, 1994). Since the end users are the ones who will be using our software, so ensuring a delightful experience for them is what is required and prototype definitely solves this purpose to a great extent. It is extremely important to meet the needs of the users (Nielson, 1993). Another important aspect is "Expectation Setting" which implies setting the expectations of our end users really high and this solely depends on how well our prototype speaks for us (Meyers & Rosson, 1992).

To understand how much importance UI/UX designing play, let's take an example of two very famous ecommerce applications, Flipkart and Amazon. They provide similar services and features but their usage varies a lot depending on their user interface designing. There can be a user who is comfortable with Flipkart but not with Amazon clearly indicating the importance of one's experience of using the application.

This leads us to a very important point. What is the one thing that the developers must always keep in mind while creating an application? Create a simple application and simple here implies that as soon as a user opens the software, he knows what to do. It sounds easy but it definitely isn't. The biggest challenge here is to think from the perspective of the user and not the developer. This again indicates the need for a prototype (Wilson &b Rosenberg, 1988).

This paper addresses the analysis of various application's interfaces in order to understand various concepts. The first three sections describe the various prototyping tools and their key features. The fourth section gives an overview of the analysis of these prototyping tools. The fifth section shows illustrative examples and the sixth will describe the prototype we have made by analysing all the aspects of interface designing including the functionalities of different graphic designing softwares like Adobe Photoshop, Adobe Illustrator along with interactive applications like Fluid UI and Wire Flow. This will enable the developers to design interactive interfaces with ease (Floyd, 2003).

DESIGNING USING ADOBE ILLUSTRATOR

Illustrator is superior in many ways in user interface creation and vector artwork. Although it is more time taking, but the interfaces created in this tool are exactly the same as the designer wants and are of very high quality. However, if there are any files or images which are imported in an illustrator project, dependencies are created. Thus, moving these files will lead to dependency errors in the project. The following are some of the reasons why one should use Adobe illustrator as a prototyping tool.

Reasons:

a) **Object Based Workflow:** Since Illustrator is the free form of object-based process, so every object can be selected and manipulated independently reducing the effort of clicking on the object's layer to select it or having to place the object in a separate layer. Using Illustrator, a lot of time can be saved while creating the project because of the ability to select objects directly.

b) **Artboard:** Adobe Illustrator enables one to create multi-page documents thereby reducing the number of files. Illustrator offers another benefit which is saving the computer's memory storage along with time as the already existing elements can be reused for different artboards eliminating the need to look for and open other files to do this.

c) **Guides:** Guides are very useful when aligning objects and shapes. They appear as lines in the workspace which help designers to quickly create layouts of their design. Also, we can convert guides into vector objects to help us with our design.

d) **Pixel Precision:** Pixel perfect designs can be made using Illustrator with a lot of settings and functions. In the beginning of any project, the size of the layout has to be mentioned with various other options to help designers make layouts exactly as they want.

e) **Gradient Fill:** Any object or shape can be filled using gradient fills. The type of gradient as well as various colors can be mentioned which can be controlled with the help of a Gradient Annotator.

DESIGNING USING ADOBE PHOTOSHOP

Adobe Photoshop is an excellent tool in creating interfaces as it overcome some of the major issues faced in illustrator. There are no dependency issues and the layouts can be made very quickly. It is a great tool for making high quality images of layouts but there is no feature of wire-framing which is a major drawback in the tool. The following are some of the features of Photoshop which illustrates why one should use it.

a) **Move Tool:** The move tool allows you to move objects. You can select layers with it, so if each of your objects is on a separate layer, this tool will move those objects just by clicking on them and dragging.

b) **Measure Tool**: Let's you measure length, width, angle and location of areas in your image. If you scan something in a little crookedly, use this tool to measure the angle and then use "rotate canvas" to correct the rotation by the exact amount.

c) **Magnetic Lasso:** For shapes that contrast with the background, this tool will snap to the edge when making a selection. Double click on the magnetic lasso icon to open the dialog box. You can set the strength of the "magnet" by entering values in the dialog box.

DESIGNING USING FLUID UI

Fluid UI is a browser-based wire-framing and prototyping tool developed by Fluid Software and used to design mobile touch interfaces. It provides the following –

a) **Built in Libraries:** Choose from 16+ libraries or upload your own images from Photoshop or the web. Create and save your own design patterns for later re-use.

b) **Gestures and Transitions:** Add taps, swipes and other gestures, then link them together and select your animations to recreate an authentic mobile, web or desktop experience.

c) **Collaboration and Feedback:** Share mockups with clients, users and stakeholders. Get crucial feedback and iterate your designs long before writing a single line of code.

d) **Flexible Archiving:** Archive all of your projects and control who has access to them. Clone entire projects to manage and maintain different versions.

Fluid UI is an ideal software that definitely makes one's life easier. It is very easy to use. Anyone who doesn't have coding knowledge can also design interfaces with ease using Fluid UI

ANALYSIS

User interface designing can be done by any of the prototyping tool mentioned above. However, it is very necessary to identify the advantages and disadvantages of each with respect to certain parameters. The following two tables describe the parameters and analysis of the different prototyping tools that we are using to analyse.

Table 1 shows the different parameters we are taken to analyse the different tools as per the requirement of the user. While designing the prototype these different parameters will help to select best selector. These parameters are used to find out differences between the different prototyping tools and for creating a difference table.

Table 1. Parameters

Parameters	Description
EventHandling	It is the receipt of an event at some event handler from an event producer and subsequent processes.
Widget Behavior	It is an element of a graphical user interface that displays information or provides a specific way for a user to interact.
Transitions	Swipe, tap or double tap, slide features.
Navigation Flowchart	Building connected multi-screen prototypes.
Dynamic Data	Information that is asynchronously changed as further updates to the information become available.
Create Shapes	Features for creating shapes.
Drag and Drop	User able to drag and drop widgets, labels, layouts etc.
Predesigned Templates	Availability of dummy templates.

Table 2. Difference table

Parameters		Adobe Photoshop	Adobe Illustrator	Fluid UI
Free Plan	**Plan**	Yes	Yes	Yes
Event Handling	**Interactivity**	No	No	Yes, Mobile
Transitions		No	No	Yes
Widget Behavior		No	No	Yes
Navigation Flowchart		No	No	Yes
Dynamic Data		No	No	No
Scripting		No	No	No
Create Shapes	**Features**	Yes	Yes	No
Drag and Drop		Yes	Yes	Yes
Predesigned Templates		No	Yes	Yes

In table 2 we analysis these different parameters on the basis of two methods ie plan, interactivity and features .Than we are going to compare these methods and parameters on the basis of different tools Adobe Photoshop, Adobe Illustrator and fluid UI. As we seen in table 2 shows the analysis of different prototyping tools on the basis of certain parameters.

ILLUSTRATIVE EXAMPLE

As per the framework of the tools different demos are created to show the difference between these tools.

To design the login layout best of the tool feature are used. In drawer layout one of the issue is inbuilt libraries the font is same. We cannot increase and decrease the font issue while working.

Description of the Table 3 and Table 4 as follows:-

In figure (a) in table 3 and 4, the layout was made with Fluid UI (Free Version). The shapes were made using drag and drop feature with built in libraries. The text font could not be changed. Images along with icons could not be added. Wire framing was made for each click on the layout to different screens.

In figure (b) in table 3 and 4, the layout was made using Adobe Illustrator with all possible customizations. Icons and Images could be added with varying sizes. Wire framing was not possible in Illustrator. In figure (c) in table 3 and 4, the layout was made with Adobe Photoshop with all possible customizations similar to Illustrator.

Figure 1. Drawer Layouts.

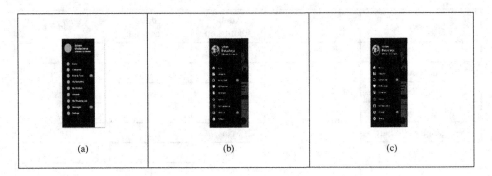

Figure 2. Login layouts

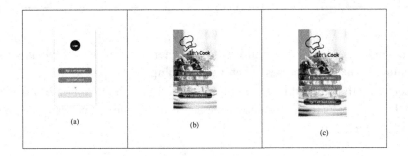

PROPOSED PROTOTYPE

The proposed prototype aims at supporting a set of features to enhance the design process of a mobile application and help designers to create interfaces rapidly and efficiently (Smith, 1995). The prototype is made for android platform and is available at Google Playstore. Some of the features are mentioned below:

a) **Sign and Registration along with Facebook Signup:** The user can have an account where he can save all his projects containing the user interfaces for various applications. All these projects are saved in the application as well in the server. The user just has to sync if he logs in from another mobile. Facebook login makes it more simple for the user to sign up and start using the features of the prototype. The projects can also be shared in any platform.

b) **Google Analytics:** This feature can allow developer of the prototype to know all the interactions made by the users with the prototype. It is a real time application which can also let us know how many users are currently using the application ad know their interaction. This can help the developer to identify user patterns and identify crashes and exceptions.

c) **GCM Push Notification:** This feature allows the developer to send information or banner advertisements through notifications to the users of the prototype.

d) **Workspace**: A series of features to enhance the development of user interfaces which includes shapes, color, Brush, adding text, eraser and many more. Along with creation of user interfaces, user can link one interface to another interface enabling wire framing in the prototype.

e) **Save in any Format:** The images made in the prototype can be saved in different format like jpeg, png or any other. The default format is jpeg.

f) **Create Layout of any Dimensions (Pixels):** When the user creates a project, he can mention the dimensions of the user interfaces he wishes to make for. This can help designers to make objects with respect to the size of the interface.

g) **Material Design**: The prototype is made with updated features of android platform and material design supporting new themes, widgets and libraries providing a new style of the application for better interactivity.

Fig 1 shows the process of login in the application. The user can either sign in manually or using Facebook. In both cases, the user will be registered in our server and can proceed to the home screen.

Fig 2 shows the process of creation of a layout. In the home screen, user will be able to see all his projects. User can create a project and enter details like layout dimensions, name and description. After this, user can start creating layouts using all the tools available in the application and save accordingly.

In table 5 Figure (a) shows the sign up screen. User can create his account by registering hi name or through Facebook. This will allow users to maintain their projects in phone as well as on cloud. Figure (b) is the workspace where user can create a user interface. Figure (c) shows the editing tools for the user to edit interfaces.

Figure 3. Login process

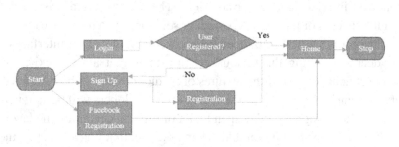

Figure 4. Interface creation process

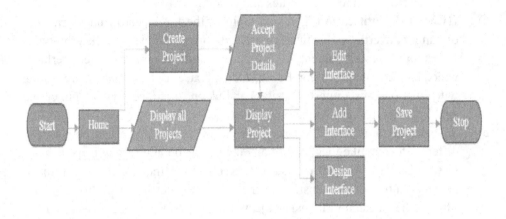

Figure 5. Layouts of the prototype

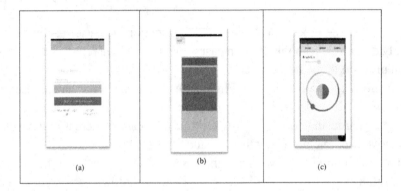

(a)   (b)   (c)

RESULT AND CONCLUSION

With this Book chapter, Authors have developed a deep understanding regarding how important user interface can be for any field. The user experience is the deciding factor for the success or failure of a particular software. As a result, we have created a prototyping tool that will help the developers create interactive interfaces.

After deeply studying the various existing tools that already exist, authorrs come to the conclusion that if the features of all these tools can be combined and a new software can be created, then the lives of the developers will be so much more easy. The graphic designers today spend a lot of time on designing the layouts and deciding how the app should look like. Using the tool that I have created, they can experiment a lot easily and designing wont be a problem at all.

FUTURE ENHANCEMENT

The future of this field is immense as everything today is technology driven. Technology has become an integral part of each individual's life. So this project can be expanded further and taken to different dimensions where a lot more features can be added in this prototyping tool.

REFERENCES

Appiah, S., Benites, P., Chang, R., & Geleg, T. (2018). *UI/UX Proposal for the Montgomery County Department of Health and Human Services.* PALS.

Bäumer, D., Bischofberger, W. R., Lichter, H., & Züllighoven, H. (1996, May). User interface prototyping—concepts, tools, and experience. In *Proceedings of the 18th international conference on Software engineering* (pp. 532-541). IEEE Computer Society. 10.1109/ICSE.1996.493447

Bernal-Cárdenas, C., Moran, K., Tufano, M., Liu, Z., Nan, L., Shi, Z., & Poshyvanyk, D. (2019, May). Guigle: a GUI search engine for Android apps. In *Proceedings of the 41st International Conference on Software Engineering: Companion Proceedings* (pp. 71-74). IEEE Press.

Chen, S., Fan, L., Chen, C., Su, T., Li, W., Liu, Y., & Xu, L. (2019, May). Storydroid: Automated generation of storyboard for Android apps. In *Proceedings of the 41st International Conference on Software Engineering* (pp. 596-607). IEEE Press.

de Lima Salgado, A., Rodrigues, S. S., & Fortes, R. P. M. (2016, September). Evolving Heuristic Evaluation for multiple contexts and audiences: Perspectives from a mapping study. In *Proceedings of the 34th ACM International Conference on the Design of Communication* (p. 19). ACM. 10.1145/2987592.2987617

De Sá, M., & Carriço, L. (2009, September). A mobile tool for in-situ prototyping. In *Proceedings of the 11th International Conference on Human-Computer Interaction with Mobile Devices and Services* (p. 20). ACM.

Floyd, C. (1984). A systematic look at prototyping. In *Approaches to prototyping* (pp. 1–18). Berlin: Springer. doi:10.1007/978-3-642-69796-8_1

Floyd, C. (1984). A systematic look at prototyping. In *Approaches to prototyping* (pp. 1–18). Berlin: Springer. doi:10.1007/978-3-642-69796-8_1

Hackos, J. T., & Redish, J. (1998). *User and task analysis for interface design.* Academic Press.

Hix, D., & Hartson, H. R. (1993). *Developing user interfaces: ensuring usability through product & process*. John Wiley & Sons, Inc.

Ismirle, J. (2018, August). Using Experience Maps to Consider Individual Stories. In *Proceedings of the 36th ACM International Conference on the Design of Communication* (p. 18). ACM. 10.1145/3233756.3233954

Isreal, J. B., & Lee, M. D. (2001). *U.S. Patent No. 6,330,007*. Washington, DC: U.S. Patent and Trademark Office.

Jitnupong, B., & Jirachiefpattana, W. (2018). Information system user interface design in software services organization: a small-clan case study. In *MATEC Web of Conferences* (*Vol. 164*, p. 01006). EDP Sciences. 10.1051/matecconf/201816401006

Landay, J. A., & Myers, B. A. (1994). *Interactive sketching for the early stages of user interface design (No. CMU-CS-94-176)*. Carnegie-Mellon Univ Pittsburgh PA Dept of Computer Science. doi:10.21236/ADA285339

Liu, T. F., Craft, M., Situ, J., Yumer, E., Mech, R., & Kumar, R. (2018, October). Learning design semantics for mobile apps. In *The 31st Annual ACM Symposium on User Interface Software and Technology* (pp. 569-579). ACM.

Marcus, A., & Gould, E. W. (2000). Crosscurrents: cultural dimensions and global Web user-interface design. *Interactions, 7*(4), 32-46.

Mirsch, T., Lehrer, C., & Jung, R. (2018). *Making Digital Nudging Applicable: The Digital Nudge Design Method*. Academic Press.

Moran, K., Bernal-Cárdenas, C., Curcio, M., Bonett, R., & Poshyvanyk, D. (2018). *Machine learning-based prototyping of graphical user interfaces for mobile apps*. arXiv preprint arXiv:1802.02312

Moran, K., Li, B., Bernal-Cárdenas, C., Jelf, D., & Poshyvanyk, D. (2018, May). Automated reporting of GUI design violations for mobile apps. In *Proceedings of the 40th International Conference on Software Engineering* (pp. 165-175). ACM. 10.1145/3180155.3180246

Moran, K., Li, B., Bernal-Cárdenas, C., Jelf, D., & Poshyvanyk, D. (2018, May). Automated reporting of GUI design violations for mobile apps. In *Proceedings of the 40th International Conference on Software Engineering* (pp. 165-175). ACM. 10.1145/3180155.3180246

Myers, B., Hudson, S. E., & Pausch, R. (2000). Past, present, and future of user interface software tools. *ACM Transactions on Computer-Human Interaction, 7*(1), 3–28.

Myers, B. A., & Rosson, M. B. (1992, June). Survey on user interface programming. In *Proceedings of the SIGCHI conference on Human factors in computing systems* (pp. 195-202). ACM. 10.1145/142750.142789

Nielsen, J. (1993). Iterative user-interface design. *Computer*, *26*(11), 32–41. doi:10.1109/2.241424

Oppermann, R. (2002). User-interface design. In *Handbook on information technologies for education and training* (pp. 233–248). Berlin: Springer. doi:10.1007/978-3-662-07682-8_15

Sharp, H. (2003). *Interaction design*. John Wiley & Sons.

Smith, S. L., & Mosier, J. N. (1986). *Guidelines for designing user interface software (No. MTR-10090)*. Bedford, MA: Mitre Corporation. doi:10.21236/ADA177198

Smith, W. R. (1995, October). Using a prototype-based language for user interface: The Newton project's experience. In OOPSLA (Vol. 95, pp. 61-72). Academic Press.

Snyder, C. (2003). *Paper prototyping: The fast and easy way to design and refine user interfaces*. Morgan Kaufmann.

Szekely, P. (1994, May). User interface prototyping: Tools and techniques. In *Workshop on Software Engineering and Human-Computer Interaction* (pp. 76-92). Springer.

Wilson, J., & Rosenberg, D. (1988). Rapid prototyping for user interface design. In *Handbook of human-computer interaction* (pp. 859–875). North-Holland. doi:10.1016/B978-0-444-70536-5.50044-0

Wood, L. E. (1997). *User interface design: Bridging the gap from user requirements to design*. CRC Press.

Chapter 9
Improving Financial Estimation in Construction Management Through Advanced Computing and Decision Making

Varun Gupta
University of Beira Interior, Covilha, Portugal

Aditya Raj Gupta
Amity University, Noida, India

Utkarsh Agrawal
Amity University, Noida, India

Ambika Kumar
Amity University, Noida, India

Rahul Verma
Amity University, Noida, India

ABSTRACT

The firm or the government invites bids against the tender whenever it requires third party to provide services to it like undertaking construction projects, delivery of material, etc. Interested parties gives their bid prices in sealed envelopes and the lowest bid rate wins the contract. However, contractor, in order to win the contract, may not estimate the cost of the project accurately as the estimation of factors contributing to the costs may be based on educated guesswork according to the past experiences. This increases the chances of the final cost of the project to go up in the end, which is to be borne by contractor. Hence, accurate and effective cost estimation is required. This chapter proposed an algorithm to provide a proper way for the contractors to estimate the accurate cost of the project for which they provide bids. This chapter provides an effective solution to the problem of inaccurate cost estimation. The algorithms are automated using a web-based tool.

DOI: 10.4018/978-1-5225-9659-2.ch009

INTRODUCTION

When an tender for undertaking activity related to projects are released, inviting bids, there are many contractors that would like to bid for it. The contractor must be technically and financially stable to compete for the specific project. Usually, the one with the lowest bid wins the tender. The cost specified by contractor is sometimes based educated guess work, which leads to cost overruns during the course of project development. This educated guess work comes from the past experiences of the company and similar projects done. Not accurately identifying the elements of the cost and risks leads to the higher final cost of the project than what was estimated earlier. Accurate cost estimation and completing the project within estimated cost leads to higher success (Aziz, Memon, Rahman, Latif & Nagapan, 2012). It had been reported that the on average the cost overrun in projects is 5–10% of project cost (Azis et al, 2012). It had also been identified that the cost and time over run is approximately 5–10% of contract duration and price of project (Rahman, Memon, Nagapan, Latif, & Azis, 2012).

An accurate and effective cost estimation is required to avoid the mismatch between estimated cost and actual costs. Further, the bids obtained by the firm (that invited it) provides it an opportunity to further lower the project cost and increase quality of work by awarding contract as subcontracts to contractors, on basis of lower elements of cost specified in bids. There are various factors that are taken into account while doing the cost estimation of a project like - the cost of the labor, cost of machinery, land cost, and type of project, resources, etc, which varies from project to project and firm to firm. To illustrate the working of the proposed algorithms, the cost factors used are generic across many contractors. These contractors was interviewed by authors to identify generic parameters that make up the cost. The different factors affecting time and cost of the project is reported in (Potty, Irdus & Ramanathan, 2001). However, to consider multiple cost factors, the algorithm is well adoptable to accommodate the extra variables.

This chapter proposed two algorithms, first; to lower the cost of projects by awarding subcontracts and second; to have effective and accurate cost estimation of the project, which can help the contractors in their endeavor of effective construction management. The first algorithm does not employ any expert judgment except that contractor may use expert judgment for cost estimation. Second algorithm may employ expert judgment and historical values to update the estimated weights. The partial application of expert judgment helps to incorporate the domain expertise of experts and consider the variability issues and overconfidence issues related to expert judgment as reported in (Azis et al, 2012).

Proposed Algorithm

Algorithm 1 (Minimizing Project Cost)

This algorithm computes the project cost on the basis of the addition of minimum factors comprising the project cost. Thus the tender is not awarded to single contractor on basis of the lowest price but sub contracts are given on basis of lowest values quoted per factor. Input factors of just factors are the one that a contractor takes into account for the estimation of the project cost. This chapter considers four hypothetical factors as the basis of the algorithm development.

For the ease of the implementation, it is assumed that there are four input factors that greatly affect the cost of the project namely F1, F2, F3, and F4. The government will ask the contractors to give the cost of all the individual four factors. From the data given, the government has to select the best contractor for the projects depending upon these factors that affect the cost. For this algorithm would provide government, the analysis for the cost of all the factors given by the contractors. Depending upon the analysis it selects the contractors that could provide the lowest value for the factors F1, F2, F3, and F4. When the cost of all these factors would be added the overall cost of the project will go down. So to give the minimum value of all the factors, the researchers considered the following:

- The duration of the project is of D days,
  F1 value is calculated on per day basis, cost per day R1
  F2 value is calculated on per day basis, cost per day R2
  F3 value is calculated on per piece basis, cost per piece R3
  F4 value is calculated on per month basis, cost per month R4

Now when all the contractors quote their price for each of the factors then the minimum of all is taken. These minimum values are then multiplied with their units and duration D.

Total cost of Factor (F1) (Cf(i)) = Minimum (Quotes of all the contractor for F1)
 * R1 * D
Total project cost = Σ Cf(i), for I = 1 to 4.

Similarly, the total cost of all the other factors can be calculated. Hence the government would be benefited by this algorithm and contracts would be given not for the entire project but only on the factor basis.

Algorithm 2

The second algorithm is given to:

(a) determine the factor whose cost is calculated incorrectly and is causing the difference in the predicted and the final cost of the project. This is based on actual data.

(b) make a better estimation for the factors by indicating the amount of variation in the predicted and final cost. This may employ expert judgment for updation of the calculated weights.

This method uses various weights as a variable assigned to the four assumed factors F1, F2, F3, and F4. These variation weights will show negative and positive value depending upon the difference between the predicted and final cost.

The positive or negative values of the variable weights given on the basis of the following:-

- If Predicted Rate, P < Actual Rate, A
  - Then negative value will be given to the weight.
- If Predicted Rate, P = Actual Rate, A
  - Then positive value will be given to the weight.
- If Predicted Rate, P > Actual Rate, A up to a defined range.
  - Then positive value will be given to the weight.
- If Predicted Rate, P >> Actual Rate, A beyond the defined range.
  - Then negative value will be given to the weight.

This method can help by indicating (a) if a factor is incorrectly predicted, (b) how much is the variation between the weights for a factor F1 when multiple values of various weights are taken over the time. The variation weights calculated are added up to the previous weight value for the final estimation.

The range of the various weights is taken from 1 to positive (n) for positive variation, and from -1 to negative (n) for negative variation. So greater the variation, lower will be the value of the weight according to the range and vice versa.

EXAMPLE (ALGORITHM 1)

Consider the following project constraints. Consider that three companies namely A, B and C decides to bid for a contract using four factors of project cost. The values per factor for each company and total cost calculated by each company are given below.

T: Duration of the project(in days), assume to be 1, for the sake of simplicity.

N: Number of units of some material, which is assumed to be 1, for the sake of simplicity.

F1: Cost Factor 1 / per day.

F2: Cost Factor 2 / per day.

F3: Cost Factor 3 / per day.

F4: Cost Factor 4 / per unit.

Company A

F1: Rs. 1/per day.

F2: Rs. 1/per day.

F3: Rs. 3/ per day.

F4: Rs. 1/per unit.

Company B

F1: Rs. 2/per day.

F2: Rs. 2/per day.

F3: Rs. 1/ per day.

F4: Rs. 2/per unit.

Company C

F1: Rs. 3/per day.

F2: Rs. 3/per day.

F3: Rs. 2/ per day.

F4: Rs. 3/per unit.

Total Cost = 1 + 1 + 1 + 1 = 4. (Recall T and N are assumed to be 1)

Thus government has to pay cost of Rs 4 only as compared to RS 6 to contractor company A (Company A has lowest bid compared to others). Using suitable data, algorithm 2 could also executed.

TOOL SUPPORT

A web application has been developed to execute the proposed algorithms. The web application can be used by the contractor to submit their bid for any project which is invited by government or any other firm. The web application also gives

Figure 1. Lowest values of cost factors

the option to the government/firm to select the different contractor for the different activities to be performed in the single project, for example labor services or machinery deployment etc. The application was names as **E-Tendrz.** The working of the application is shown below with the help of the screenshot.

Figure 1 shows the lowest bids of all factors of all contractors, thereby resulting in reduction in project cost to government and hence profit to them.

CONCLUSION

This chapter suggest an cost estimation algorithms that will help the construction company to predict the cost of the project close to the actual cost and for the firm inviting tenders to lower the cost at which tender is awarded. Tender is awarded at low cost because now it is not awarded to single contractor on basis of the lowest price but sub contracts are given on basis of lowest values quoted per factor. This algorithms with the ability to consider the ratings of the contractor will give a system the ability to increase the accuracy of the predicted cost of a project, help bring the overall cost of the project down effectively and select a contractor which has a history of completing the project in given time, budget and with good quality. Therefore, this innovative system can improve the current practices followed throughout the industry in a simple and efficient way. The evaluation of algorithm 2 on live data set, is kept as future work.

REFERENCES

Azis, A. A. A., Memon, A. H., Rahman, I. A., Latif, Q. B. A. I., & Nagapan, S. (2012, September). Cost management of large construction projects in South Malaysia. In *2012 IEEE Symposium on Business, Engineering and Industrial Applications* (pp. 625-629). IEEE. 10.1109/ISBEIA.2012.6422964

Faria, P., & Miranda, E. (2012, October). Expert Judgment in Software Estimation During the Bid Phase of a Project--An Exploratory Survey. In *2012 Joint Conference of the 22nd International Workshop on Software Measurement and the 2012 Seventh International Conference on Software Process and Product Measurement* (pp. 126-131). IEEE. 10.1109/IWSM-MENSURA.2012.27

Potty, N. S., Irdus, A. B., & Ramanathan, C. T. (2011, September). Case study and survey on time and cost overrun of multiple D&B projects. In *2011 National Postgraduate Conference* (pp. 1-6). IEEE. 10.1109/NatPC.2011.6136364

Rahman, I. A., Memon, A. H., Nagapan, S., Latif, Q. B. A. I., & Azis, A. A. A. (2012, December). Time and cost performance of costruction projects in southern and cenrtal regions of Penisular Malaysia. In *2012 IEEE Colloquium on Humanities, Science and Engineering (CHUSER)* (pp. 52-57). IEEE. 10.1109/CHUSER.2012.6504280

Chapter 10

Independent Verification and Validation of FPGA-Based Design for Airborne Electronic Applications

Sudha Srinivasan
Aeronautical Development Agency (ADA), Bangalore, India

D. S. Chauhan
GLA University, Mathura, India

Rekha R.
Aeronautical Development Agency (ADA), Bangalore, India

ABSTRACT

Field programmable gate arrays (FPGAs) are finding increasing number of applications in high integrity safety critical systems of aerospace and defence industry. Though FPGA design goes through various development processes, it is widely observed that the critical errors are observed in the final stages of development, thereby impacting time and cost. The risk of failure in complex embedded systems is overcome by using the independent verification and validation (IV&V) technique. Independent verification and validation (IV&V) of FPGA-based design is essential for evaluating the correctness, quality, and safety of the airborne embedded systems throughout the development life cycle and provides early detection and identification of risk elements. The process of IV&V and its planning needs to be initiated early in the development life cycle. This chapter describes the IV&V methodology for FPGA-based design during the development life cycle along with the certification process.

DOI: 10.4018/978-1-5225-9659-2.ch010

INTRODUCTION

Complex custom micro-coded components are becoming increasingly popular for use in high integrity safety critical systems. These complex custom micro-coded components include Application Specific Integrated Circuits (ASIC), Programmable Logic Devices (PLD), Field Programmable Gate Arrays (FPGA), or similar electronic components used in the design of aircraft systems. The extensive use of these Complex custom micro-coded components results in development and certification challenges. Hence, it's necessary to overcome these challenges to ensure that the potential for design errors is addressed in a more consistent and verifiable manner during both the development and certification phases.

Field Programmable Gate Arrays (FPGAs) are becoming more popular for use within high integrity and safety critical systems. FPGAs contain millions of programmable logic cells, which can be configured for a wide variety of tasks, and offer many benefits over traditional micro-processors, such as efficient parallel processing and very predictable performance.

FPGAs are configured using a Hardware Description Language (HDL), such as the VHDL (VHSIC Very High Speed Integrated Circuit Hardware Description Language), Verilog and System C to describe the required logic. This is converted into a configuration file which is loaded onto the FPGA device. DO-254 (RTCA/DO-254, 2000) guideline provides design assurance guidance for the development of airborne electronic hardware such that it shall safely performs its intended function, in its specified environments. However, DO-254 guideline is applicable to Line Replacement units, Circuit Board Assemblies, Custom micro-coded components, such as Application Specific Integrated Circuits (ASICs) and Programmable Logic Devices (PLD) and does not explicitly bring out the IV&V of development life cycle of FPGA based design.

This paper brings out the IV&V activities to be carried out during the FPGA development life cycle starting from planning phase to certification.

BACKGROUND

From references, (RTCA/DO-254, 2000) describes Design Assurance Guidance for Airborne Electronics Hardware for Line Replacement Units (LRUs), Circuit Board Assemblies, ASICs, PLDs, Integrated technology components such as hybrids and multichip modules and COTS components. (DoT FAA, 2015) focuses on the verification process and verification tools used for airborne electronic hardware (AEH) devices such as Field Programmable Gate Array (FPGAs), programmable logic devices (PLD) and application specific integrated circuits (ASICs).

Dagan (2011) Gives the practical use of FPGAs and IP in DO-254 compliant systems and defines COTS devices as components, integrated circuits, or subsystems that are developed by a supplier for multiple customers, whose design and configuration are controlled by the specification from the suppliers or industry, (RTCA DO-254 CAST-33, 2014) is a CAST paper for airborne COTS IP used in PLD and ASICs and is an acceptable means of compliance for Programmable Logic Devices (PLDs) and Application Specific Integrated Circuits (ASICs) implementing a third party Commercial Off-The-Shelf (COTS) Intellectual Properties (IP).

Paul and Anthony (2009) focuses on selecting the Ideal FPGA vendor for Military programs, Keithan (2008) is an advisory circular released by FAA and describes the design assurance for complex custom micro-coded components with hardware design assurance levels. Tasiran and Keutzer (2001) is a whitepaper focusing the verification process and verification tools for airborne electronic hardware (AEH). Liu and Jou (2001) describes the Advanced Verification Methods for Safety-Critical Airborne Electronic Hardware. (CYIENT, 2015) focuses on coverage metrics for Functional and Code coverage. Ref(j)elaborates on verifying the correctness of the initial Register Transfer Language(RTL) descriptions written in hardware description language(HDL) and the six different types of coverage metrics i.e. Statement, Block, decision, path, event and FSM. Discusses the key technical challenges involved in V&V of FPGA in the Aerospace and Defence Industry and highlights on how a global partnership can help optimize FPGA development by driving innovation, optimizing cost, and providing access to resources in emerging markets like India.

None of the above papers have addressed the life cycle activities for performing a thorough Independent Verification and Validation of FPGA based systems for airborne applications leading to certification for flight. Section 3 presents a brief detail of FPGA Development Life Cycle. Section 4 gives the IV&V methods and techniques for FPGA. It lists the IV&V activities to be carried out for the FPGA development life cycle that includes planning phase, requirement phase, detailed design phase, implementation phase and certification phase.

FPGA DEVELOPMENT LIFE CYCLE

The FPGA development life cycle is equally applicable to the development of new systems or equipment and modifications to existing systems or equipment. The FPGA design life cycle processes may be iterative, that is entered, re-entered and modified due to incremental development and feedback between the processes.

The Figure: 1 shows phases of the entire FPGA development life cycle processes:

Figure 1. Phases of FPGA Development Life Cycle

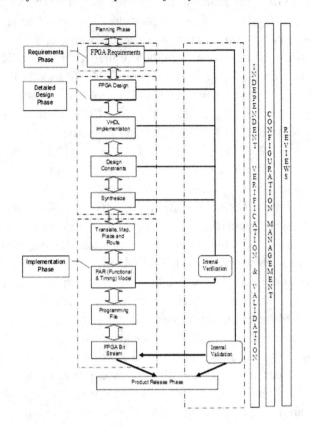

Planning Phase

The purpose of the FPGA planning phase is to define the means of producing FPGA Design which will satisfy the functional requirements. Effective planning is required to produce good FPGA Design. Checklist for entire Life Cycle is to be prepared along with the IV&V team and Certification Agency during the planning phase. To initiate planning phase FPGA Top Level Requirement Specifications, Interface Requirement Specifications and System Safety Assessment Results are mandatory. Planning documents namely Plan for FPGA Aspects for Certification, FPGA Design Plan, FPGA Configuration Management Plan and FPGA Verification Plan are generated for each sub-system / project.

FPGA Requirement Phase

The FPGA requirements capture process identifies and records the hardware item requirements for FPGA design implementation and its working under safety critical regions. This includes those derived requirements imposed by the FPGA architecture, choice of technology, the basic and optional functionality, environmental, and performance requirements as well as the requirements imposed by the system safety assessment. This process may be iterative since additional requirements may become known during design.

FPGA Requirement Phase is initiated once System Functional Architecture Document, Plan for FPGA Aspects for Certification, FPGA Design Plan, FPGA Configuration Management Plan and FPGA Verification Plan are prepared.

During this phase, FPGA Detailed Requirement Specification, External Interface Document, FPGA Test Plan and Requirement Traceability Matrix is prepared. The system requirements allocated to the FPGA shall be documented. These may include identifying requirements, such as functionality and performance, and architectural considerations, Built-In-Test, testability and maintenance considerations, power and physical characteristics and documented in FPGA Detailed Requirement Specification. It shall identify and record the external interface requirements in External Interface Document. This includes those requirements imposed by the IP architecture, IP controllability and configuration, environmental, safety and performance requirements.

Traceability from FPGA Detailed Requirement Specification to FPGA test plan shall be documented in Requirement Traceability Matrix. FPGA Test Plan shall include all requirements from FPGA Detailed Requirement Specifications to be tested.

FPGA Detailed Design Phase

FPGA design is the intermediate and essential activity between requirements and implementation. The complexity and criticality of the FPGA is to be assessed and appropriate design methodology has to be chosen. A conceptual design phase becomes essential for very complex systems where various implementation options are to be explored to determine the optimum and maintainable design. The detailed design phase extends the FPGA architecture defined in the conceptual design.

Planning phase outputs such as Plan for FPGA Aspects of Certification and FPGA Design Plan along with requirement phase output artifacts are required to commence FPGA detailed Design Phase. FPGA Design Data document is prepared that includes Conceptual design data, Reliability, maintenance and test features, preliminary FPGA safety assessment data, Design Constraints and Hardware/Software Interface Data.

VHDL has been used for in the project. However, since all the features of VHDL cannot be used for safety critical systems development, it is essential that a safe subset of the language should be used. In this regard, IV&V formulated a safe subset of coding rules for development of airborne safety critical systems based on Mentor Graphics, ALDEC and STARC coding standards. The following rationales were implemented for programming using VHDL. The developed code was found efficient and error free.

R1: Design should not have Clock Domain Crossing (CDC). Meta-stability is a serious problem in safety-critical designs, which frequently causes chips to exhibit intermittent failures. These failures generally go undetected during simulation (which tests a chip's logic functions) and static timing analysis (which tests for timing within a single clock domain).

R2: Design should not have set up, hold time violations and clock skew. This can be run at various phases in the design process like translate, map, Place & Route. Static Timing Analysis (STA) gives the information about setup and hold time violations and clock skew.

R3: Design should not have unsafe synthesis. Safe Synthesis is checked to ensure that a proper net list is created by the synthesis tool. If this is violated in some cases the pre-synthesis RTL simulations will not match the post synthesis gate level simulations.

R4: Design reviews and code comprehension should not be cumbersome. The design reviews and code comprehension should be source level transparent, verifiable, maintainable and readable and include those attributes that facilitates the understanding of the software by project personnel. Code should have a formal syntax.

An example of coding rule with rationale is given below

RULE: Do not use flip-flop output as a clock.

Rule Description

Do not use a flip-flop output as a clock or input to itself - avoid internally generated clocks as much as possible unless they are isolated properly.

Rationale: R1, R2&R3

Example Showing Violation of the Rule

In the VHDL Code given below, the output of the first flip-flop 'dout' is used as a clock to the next flip-flop. The following code in figure 2and figure 3 shows the VHDL Code rule and RTL schematic violation.

VHDL code for the violation:

VHDL code following Coding Rule:

Figure 2. VHDL Code with Code Rule violation

```
1   Library IEEE;
2   Use IEEE.std_logic_1164.all;
3   entity dflipflop is
4   Port (clk: in std_logic;
5   din: in std_logic;
6   dout1: out std_logic;
7   din1:std_logic);
8   end dflipflop;
9   architecture Behavioral of dflipflop is
10  signal dout : std_logic;
11  signal temp : std_logic;
12  begin
13  temp <= dout;
14  process(clk)
15  begin
16  if clk = '0' then
17  dout <= din;
18  end if;
19  end process;
20  process(dout)
21  begin
22  if(dout = '1') then
23  dout1 <= din1;
24  end if;
25  end process;
26  end Behavioral;
```

Figure 3. RTL Schematic for the violation

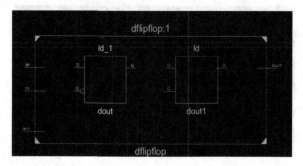

The VHDL source code for 'the output of the first flip-flop 'dout' to the next flip-flop input' being implemented as shown in figure 4 and figure 5. The clock is simultaneously given to both the flip flops.

Output artifacts of FPGA Detailed Design Phase shall include FPGA Design Data, RTL, Netlist (Synthesis and Simulation), Testbenches, Simulation Result and Code Quality Check Report.

Figure 4. VHDL Code with Coding Rule compliance

```
1   Library IEEE;
2   Use IEEE.std_logic_1164.all;
3   entity dflipflop is
4   Port (clk: in std_logic;
5   din: in std_logic;
6   dout1: out std_logic);
7   end dflipflop;
8   architecture Behavioral of dflipflop is
9   signal dout : std_logic;
10  signal temp : std_logic;
11  begin
12  temp <= dout;
13  process(clk)
14  begin
15  if clk = '0' then
16  dout <= din;
17  end if;
18  end process;
19  process(dout,clk)
20  begin
21  if clk = '0' then
22  dout1 <= dout;
23  end if;
24  end process;
25  end Behavioral;
```

Figure 5. RTL Schematic for the coding rule compliance

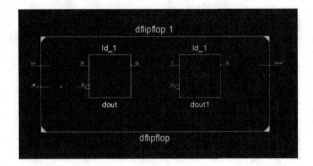

FPGA Implementation Phase

Implementation phase consists of integration of all individual designs into a single entity, mapping to the FPGA resources and Place & Route and generating the Bitstream. The designer can use any standard design debug tools or signal generators, logic analyzers, device programmers.

Implementation Phase requires FPGA Design data, Netlist, Simulation Result and Testbenches. FPGA implementation process shall use the detailed design data to produce the Bitstream, Simulation Result report, Timing analysis Report, Test Report, FPGA Accomplishment Summary and FPGA Configuration Index.

IV&V METHODS AND TECHNIQUES FOR FPGA

IV&V is a system engineering process employing rigorous methodologies for evaluating the correctness, quality and safety of the airborne embedded systems throughout the software development life cycle. It is required for the early detection and identification of risk elements. The program is then able to take actions to mitigate these risks early in the life cycle. Independent Verification and validation of FPGA based design is an ongoing process, where the intensity of V&V process that is applied is based on the design assurance levels (DAL) as specified in the DO-254. The IV&V methods and Techniques needs to be enforced for FPGA in each FPGA development life cycle phase. In each phase, the design team shall formally release the output artifacts after carrying out their internal verification and Validation. IV&V shall independently prepare observations after thoroughly analyzing all output artifacts of that phase. IV&V may also prepare interim reports during the phase to bring concerns to the attention of management.

The figure 6 shows the information interchange between development phases of FPGA and IV&V Activities for FPGA development life cycle.

IV&V of Planning Phase

The purpose of the planning phase is to define the means of designing FPGA which will satisfy the system requirements. Effective planning is a determining factor in designing FPGA. The planning documents namely Plan for FPGA Aspects of Certification, FPGA Design Plan, FPGA Configuration Management Plan, FPGA Verification Plan, are verified for each subsystem/project

Figure 6. FPGA Development Life Cycle Activities

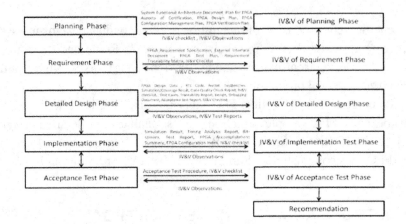

IV&V of Requirement Phase

FPGA development processes produce one or more levels of FPGA requirements. High level requirements are produced directly through analysis of system requirements and system architecture.

These high level requirements are further developed during the FPGA design process, thus producing one or more successive, lower levels of requirements. Low level requirements are FPGA requirements from which design can be directly implemented without further information.

Derived requirements are requirements that are not directly traceable to the higher level of requirements. High level requirements may include derived requirements, and low level requirements also may include derived requirements. As a part of the IV&V activity in the requirements phase, the correctness of the allocation of system requirements to software is checked along with the correctness, completeness, non-ambiguity, testability and traceability of the requirements

IV&V of Detailed Design Phase

This shall be conducted after the completion of FPGA detailed design by the designers. FPGA Design Data shall be verified to ensure that it includes High level description, all major components, Top level functional description, Design Constraints, etc. IV&V shall verify FPGA Design Data, RTL, Netlist (Synthesis and Simulation), Testbenches, Simulation Result, Code Quality Check Report.

The important activities carried out by IV&V during detailed design phase includes:

a. Manual walk through of VHDL source code.
b. Verification of Traceability report.
c. Ensuring compliance to IV&V recommended coding rules.
d. Functional Simulation to validate the timing requirements and input and output signals.
e. Timing Simulations to validate the FPGAs.

IV&V shall also perform the following activities in the detailed design phase.

Code Coverage Analysis

Code coverage analysis is one of the advanced verification approaches used to comply with the elemental analysis stated in DO-254 that requires all the elements in a design to be verified. The identified elements for coverage in the HDL code are branches, instructions, statements, conditions and toggle. IV&V shall ensure complete code coverage by including additional test cases in the existing testbenches.

Figure 7 shows the snapshot of Code coverage report of the sample project.

Verification through Waveform generation

The FPGA module designs are compiled & verified using Questa Prime tool. The sample project of FPGA based system VHDL source code is simulated and synthesized, and then the design results are verified as shown in figure 8. The waveform thus generated is analyzed for standard delay, delta delay and transport delays and wave log file (wlf) is generated that provides precise in-simulation and post-simulation debugging.

Figure 7. Code Coverage Report

Enabled Coverage	Active	Hits	Misses	% Covered
Stmts	21	20	1	95.2
Branches	14	13	1	92.8
FEC Condition Terms	0	0	0	100.0
FEC Expression Terms	0	0	0	100.0
FSMs				100.0
States	0	0	0	100.0
Transitions	0	0	0	100.0
Toggle Bins	1144	197	947	17.2

IV & V of Implementation Phase

This shall be conducted after the completion of FPGA Implementation phase by the designers. IV&V shall verify Simulation Result report, Timing analysis Report, Test Report, FPGA Accomplishment Summary and FPGA Configuration Index.

Once the bitstream is ported to the target, IV&V shall carry out the following activities:

a.   Verify IO pin toggle coverage using Testbenches
b.   Verify the FPGA Post PnR level (Timing Analysis)
c.   Carry out target level testing
d.   Ensure that test cases covers all functionalities of FPGA
e.   Ensure that test cases are traceable to requirements

CERTIFICATION PROCESS

IV&V shall Participate in Target Testing for FPGA and verify the test cases mentioned in the Acceptance Test Procedure and ensure that each test case is unique and covers all functionality of FPGA and all activities listed in IV&V checklist are covered. IV&V Team constituted by program management carries out the FPGA certification activities. This involves determining whether the FPGA development complies with the Plan for FPGA aspects of certification. Certification is accomplished by reviewing the FPGA Accomplishment Summary and evidence of compliance.

Figure 8. Generation of waveform from Netlist and Testbenches

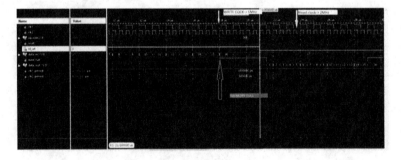

CONCLUSION

Though FPGA based development is becoming increasingly popular, the problems in FPGA development life cycle are mitigated by following important processes like:

a. Preparation and Release of Planning Documents
b. Requirement specifications with details of Functionality added or deleted or updated during development.
c. Traceability matrix across documents
d. Configuration Management

This paper describes the Independent Verification and Validation of FPGA-based Design for airborne electronic applications.

The Independent Verification and Validation of various phases of FPGA development life cycle like Planning, Requirement, Detailed design and Implementation phases are used to prove the FPGA design before integrating with the target. After successful acceptance test and certification, IV&V provides the required confidence in the FPGA based design to be used in airborne application.

The design, development, verification, validation and certification process described in this paper for FPGA-based systems is being successfully used in the Indian defence projects.

ACKNOWLEDGMENT

Much of the work reported in this paper was carried out by the principle author. The author wishes to acknowledge and thank the comments and assistance of Mr. Kulbhushan Bhaiji Patariya and Ms. Dhanaselvi D for their valuable contribution.

REFERENCES

CYIENT. (2015). *Verification and Validation of Field Programmable Gate Arrays in the Aerospace and Defence industry* (White paper). CYIENT.

Dagan, W. (2011). Practical Use of FPGA and IP in DO-254 Compliant Systems. *Xilinx Inc.* Retrieved September 8, 2011, from https://www.xilinx.com/support/documentation/white_papers/wp403_DO254_IP_Use.pdf

DoT FAA. (2015). *Advanced Verification Methods for Safety-Critical Airborne Electronic Hardware (DOT/FAA/TC-14/41).* FAA.

Keithan, J. P. (2008). The Use of Advanced Verification Methods to Address DO-254 Design Assurance. In *Proceedings of IEEE Aerospace Conference*. Big Sky, MT: IEEE. 10.1109/AERO.2008.4526684

Liu, C. N., & Jou, J. Y. (2001). Efficient coverage analysis metric for HDL design validation. *Proceedings of IEE Proceedings - Computers and Digital Technique, 148*(1), 1-6. 10.1049/ip-cdt:20010203

Paul & Stone. (2009). Understanding DO-254 Compliance for the verification of airborne digital hardware. *Synopsys Inc*. Retrieved December 2016 from https://pdfs. semanticscholar.org/f531/310a09377f0e4cb3565eb1ce49fb877a5043.pdf

RTCA DO-254 CAST-33. (2014). *Design Assurance Guidance for Airborne Electronic Hardware, for COTS Intellectual Property Used in Programmable Logic Devices and Application Specific Integrated Circuits*. RTCA.

RTCA/DO-254. (2000). *Design Assurance Guidance for Airborne Electronic Hardware*. RTCA.

Tasiran, S., & Keutzer, K. (2001). Coverage metrics for functional validation of hardware designs. In *Proceedings of IEEE Design & Test of Computers* (Vol. 18, pp. 36 – 45). Los Alamitos, CA: IEEE. 10.1109/54.936247

KEY TERMS AND DEFINITIONS

DO-254: Is a design assurance guideline for airborne electronics hardware that ensures the safe operation of complex electronics hardware to perform its intended function.

FPGA: Field programmable gate arrays consists of configurable logic blocks (CLB) that can be programmed, input output interface, and configurable interconnect that connects these blocks.

IV&V: Independent verification and validation is the set of verification and validation activities performed by an agency not under the control of the organizational unit that is developing the software.

VHDL: VHSIC, very high-speed integrated circuit hardware description language, is a programming language for hardware description language.

Related Readings

To continue IGI Global's long-standing tradition of advancing innovation through emerging research, please find below a compiled list of recommended IGI Global book chapters and journal articles in the areas of crowdsourcing, software engineering, and probabilistic decision-making. These related readings will provide additional information and guidance to further enrich your knowledge and assist you with your own research.

Abramek, E. (2019). Maturity Profiles of Organizations for Social Media. In R. Lenart-Gansiniec (Ed.), *Crowdsourcing and Knowledge Management in Contemporary Business Environments* (pp. 134–145). Hershey, PA: IGI Global. doi:10.4018/978-1-5225-4200-1.ch007

Abu Talib, M. (2018). Towards Sustainable Development Through Open Source Software in the Arab World. In M. Khosrow-Pour, D.B.A. (Ed.), Optimizing Contemporary Application and Processes in Open Source Software (pp. 222-242). Hershey, PA: IGI Global. doi:10.4018/978-1-5225-5314-4.ch009

Adesola, A. P., & Olla, G. O. (2018). Unlocking the Unlimited Potentials of Koha OSS/ILS for Library House-Keeping Functions: A Global View. In M. Khosrow-Pour, D.B.A. (Ed.), Optimizing Contemporary Application and Processes in Open Source Software (pp. 124-163). Hershey, PA: IGI Global. doi:10.4018/978-1-5225-5314-4.ch006

Akber, A., Rizvi, S. S., Khan, M. W., Uddin, V., Hashmani, M. A., & Ahmad, J. (2019). Dimensions of Robust Security Testing in Global Software Engineering: A Systematic Review. In M. Rehman, A. Amin, A. Gilal, & M. Hashmani (Eds.), *Human Factors in Global Software Engineering* (pp. 252–272). Hershey, PA: IGI Global. doi:10.4018/978-1-5225-9448-2.ch010

Amrollahi, A., & Ahmadi, M. H. (2019). What Motivates the Crowd?: A Literature Review on Motivations for Crowdsourcing. In R. Lenart-Gansiniec (Ed.), *Crowdsourcing and Knowledge Management in Contemporary Business Environments* (pp. 103–133). Hershey, PA: IGI Global. doi:10.4018/978-1-5225-4200-1.ch006

Anchitaalagammai, J. V., Samayadurai, K., Murali, S., Padmadevi, S., & Shantha Lakshmi Revathy, J. (2019). Best Practices: Adopting Security Into the Software Development Process for IoT Applications. In D. Mala (Ed.), *Integrating the Internet of Things Into Software Engineering Practices* (pp. 146–159). Hershey, PA: IGI Global. doi:10.4018/978-1-5225-7790-4.ch007

Bhavsar, S. A., Pandit, B. Y., & Modi, K. J. (2019). Social Internet of Things. In D. Mala (Ed.), *Integrating the Internet of Things Into Software Engineering Practices* (pp. 199–218). Hershey, PA: IGI Global. doi:10.4018/978-1-5225-7790-4.ch010

Biswas, A., & De, A. K. (2019). *Multi-Objective Stochastic Programming in Fuzzy Environments* (pp. 1–420). Hershey, PA: IGI Global. doi:10.4018/978-1-5225-8301-1

Callaghan, C. W. (2017). The Probabilistic Innovation Field of Scientific Enquiry. *International Journal of Sociotechnology and Knowledge Development, 9*(2), 56–72. doi:10.4018/IJSKD.2017040104

Chhabra, D., & Sharma, I. (2018). Role of Attacker Capabilities in Risk Estimation and Mitigation. In R. Kumar, A. Tayal, & S. Kapil (Eds.), *Analyzing the Role of Risk Mitigation and Monitoring in Software Development* (pp. 244–255). Hershey, PA: IGI Global. doi:10.4018/978-1-5225-6029-6.ch015

Chitra, P., & Abirami, S. (2019). Smart Pollution Alert System Using Machine Learning. In D. Mala (Ed.), *Integrating the Internet of Things Into Software Engineering Practices* (pp. 219–235). Hershey, PA: IGI Global. doi:10.4018/978-1-5225-7790-4.ch011

Dorsey, M. D., & Raisinghani, M. S. (2019). IT Governance or IT Outsourcing: Is There a Clear Winner? In A. Mukherjee & A. Krishna (Eds.), *Interdisciplinary Approaches to Information Systems and Software Engineering* (pp. 19–32). Hershey, PA: IGI Global. doi:10.4018/978-1-5225-7784-3.ch002

Dua, R., Sharma, S., & Kumar, R. (2018). Risk Management Metrics. In R. Kumar, A. Tayal, & S. Kapil (Eds.), *Analyzing the Role of Risk Mitigation and Monitoring in Software Development* (pp. 21–33). Hershey, PA: IGI Global. doi:10.4018/978-1-5225-6029-6.ch002

Dua, R., Sharma, S., & Sharma, A. (2018). Software Vulnerability Management: How Intelligence Helps in Mitigating Software Vulnerabilities. In R. Kumar, A. Tayal, & S. Kapil (Eds.), *Analyzing the Role of Risk Mitigation and Monitoring in Software Development* (pp. 34–45). Hershey, PA: IGI Global. doi:10.4018/978-1-5225-6029-6.ch003

Fatema, K., Syeed, M. M., & Hammouda, I. (2018). Demography of Open Source Software Prediction Models and Techniques. In M. Khosrow-Pour, D.B.A. (Ed.), Optimizing Contemporary Application and Processes in Open Source Software (pp. 24-56). Hershey, PA: IGI Global. doi:10.4018/978-1-5225-5314-4.ch002

Ghafele, R., & Gibert, B. (2018). Open Growth: The Economic Impact of Open Source Software in the USA. In M. Khosrow-Pour, D.B.A. (Ed.), Optimizing Contemporary Application and Processes in Open Source Software (pp. 164-197). Hershey, PA: IGI Global. doi:10.4018/978-1-5225-5314-4.ch007

Gilal, A. R., Tunio, M. Z., Waqas, A., Almomani, M. A., Khan, S., & Gilal, R. (2019). Task Assignment and Personality: Crowdsourcing Software Development. In M. Rehman, A. Amin, A. Gilal, & M. Hashmani (Eds.), *Human Factors in Global Software Engineering* (pp. 1–19). Hershey, PA: IGI Global. doi:10.4018/978-1-5225-9448-2.ch001

Gopikrishnan, S., & Priakanth, P. (2019). Web-Based IoT Application Development. In D. Mala (Ed.), *Integrating the Internet of Things Into Software Engineering Practices* (pp. 62–86). Hershey, PA: IGI Global. doi:10.4018/978-1-5225-7790-4.ch004

Guendouz, M., Amine, A., & Hamou, R. M. (2018). Open Source Projects Recommendation on GitHub. In M. Khosrow-Pour, D.B.A. (Ed.), Optimizing Contemporary Application and Processes in Open Source Software (pp. 86-101). Hershey, PA: IGI Global. doi:10.4018/978-1-5225-5314-4.ch004

Hashmani, M. A., Zaffar, M., & Ejaz, R. (2019). Scenario Based Test Case Generation Using Activity Diagram and Action Semantics. In M. Rehman, A. Amin, A. Gilal, & M. Hashmani (Eds.), *Human Factors in Global Software Engineering* (pp. 297–321). Hershey, PA: IGI Global. doi:10.4018/978-1-5225-9448-2.ch012

Jagannathan, J., & Anitha Elavarasi, S. (2019). Current Trends: Machine Learning and AI in IoT. In D. Mala (Ed.), *Integrating the Internet of Things Into Software Engineering Practices* (pp. 181–198). Hershey, PA: IGI Global. doi:10.4018/978-1-5225-7790-4.ch009

Jasmine, K. S. (2019). A New Process Model for IoT-Based Software Engineering. In D. Mala (Ed.), *Integrating the Internet of Things Into Software Engineering Practices* (pp. 1–13). Hershey, PA: IGI Global. doi:10.4018/978-1-5225-7790-4.ch001

Juma, M. F., Fue, K. G., Barakabitze, A. A., Nicodemus, N., Magesa, M. M., Kilima, F. T., & Sanga, C. A. (2017). Understanding Crowdsourcing of Agricultural Market Information in a Pilot Study: Promises, Problems and Possibilities (3Ps). *International Journal of Technology Diffusion, 8*(4), 1–16. doi:10.4018/IJTD.2017100101

Karthick, G. S., & Pankajavalli, P. B. (2019). Internet of Things Testing Framework, Automation, Challenges, Solutions and Practices: A Connected Approach for IoT Applications. In D. Mala (Ed.), *Integrating the Internet of Things Into Software Engineering Practices* (pp. 87–124). Hershey, PA: IGI Global. doi:10.4018/978-1-5225-7790-4.ch005

Kashyap, R. (2019). Big Data and Global Software Engineering. In M. Rehman, A. Amin, A. Gilal, & M. Hashmani (Eds.), *Human Factors in Global Software Engineering* (pp. 131–163). Hershey, PA: IGI Global. doi:10.4018/978-1-5225-9448-2.ch006

Kashyap, R. (2019). Systematic Model for Decision Support System. In A. Mukherjee & A. Krishna (Eds.), *Interdisciplinary Approaches to Information Systems and Software Engineering* (pp. 62–98). Hershey, PA: IGI Global. doi:10.4018/978-1-5225-7784-3.ch004

Kaur, J., & Kaur, R. (2018). Estimating Risks Related to Extended Enterprise Systems (EES). In R. Kumar, A. Tayal, & S. Kapil (Eds.), *Analyzing the Role of Risk Mitigation and Monitoring in Software Development* (pp. 118–135). Hershey, PA: IGI Global. doi:10.4018/978-1-5225-6029-6.ch008

Kaur, Y., & Singh, S. (2018). Risk Mitigation Planning, Implementation, and Progress Monitoring: Risk Mitigation. In R. Kumar, A. Tayal, & S. Kapil (Eds.), *Analyzing the Role of Risk Mitigation and Monitoring in Software Development* (pp. 1–20). Hershey, PA: IGI Global. doi:10.4018/978-1-5225-6029-6.ch001

Kavitha, S., Anchitaalagammai, J. V., Nirmala, S., & Murali, S. (2019). Current Trends in Integrating the Internet of Things Into Software Engineering Practices. In D. Mala (Ed.), *Integrating the Internet of Things Into Software Engineering Practices* (pp. 14–35). Hershey, PA: IGI Global. doi:10.4018/978-1-5225-7790-4.ch002

Köse, U. (2018). Optimization Scenarios for Open Source Software Used in E-Learning Activities. In M. Khosrow-Pour, D.B.A. (Ed.), *Optimizing Contemporary Application and Processes in Open Source Software* (pp. 102-123). Hershey, PA: IGI Global. doi:10.4018/978-1-5225-5314-4.ch005

Kumar, A., Singh, A. K., Awasthi, N., & Singh, V. (2019). Natural Hazard: Tropical Cyclone – Evaluation of HE and IMSRA Over CS KYANT. In A. Mukherjee & A. Krishna (Eds.), *Interdisciplinary Approaches to Information Systems and Software Engineering* (pp. 124–141). Hershey, PA: IGI Global. doi:10.4018/978-1-5225-7784-3.ch006

Kumar, N., Singh, S. K., Reddy, G. P., & Naitam, R. K. (2019). Developing Logistic Regression Models to Identify Salt-Affected Soils Using Optical Remote Sensing. In A. Mukherjee & A. Krishna (Eds.), *Interdisciplinary Approaches to Information Systems and Software Engineering* (pp. 233–256). Hershey, PA: IGI Global. doi:10.4018/978-1-5225-7784-3.ch010

Kumar, U., Kumar, N., Mishra, V. N., & Jena, R. K. (2019). Soil Quality Assessment Using Analytic Hierarchy Process (AHP): A Case Study. In A. Mukherjee & A. Krishna (Eds.), *Interdisciplinary Approaches to Information Systems and Software Engineering* (pp. 1–18). Hershey, PA: IGI Global. doi:10.4018/978-1-5225-7784-3.ch001

Lal, S., Sardana, N., & Sureka, A. (2018). Logging Analysis and Prediction in Open Source Java Project. In M. Khosrow-Pour, D.B.A. (Ed.), *Optimizing Contemporary Application and Processes in Open Source Software* (pp. 57-85). Hershey, PA: IGI Global. doi:10.4018/978-1-5225-5314-4.ch003

Latif, A. M., Khan, K. M., & Duc, A. N. (2019). Software Cost Estimation and Capability Maturity Model in Context of Global Software Engineering. In M. Rehman, A. Amin, A. Gilal, & M. Hashmani (Eds.), *Human Factors in Global Software Engineering* (pp. 273–296). Hershey, PA: IGI Global. doi:10.4018/978-1-5225-9448-2.ch011

Lenart-Gansiniec, R. A. (2019). Crowdsourcing as an Example of Public Management Fashion. In R. Lenart-Gansiniec (Ed.), *Crowdsourcing and Knowledge Management in Contemporary Business Environments* (pp. 1–19). Hershey, PA: IGI Global. doi:10.4018/978-1-5225-4200-1.ch001

Lukyanenko, R., & Parsons, J. (2018). Beyond Micro-Tasks: Research Opportunities in Observational Crowdsourcing. *Journal of Database Management*, 29(1), 1–22. doi:10.4018/JDM.2018010101

Mala, D. (2019). IoT Functional Testing Using UML Use Case Diagrams: IoT in Testing. In D. Mala (Ed.), *Integrating the Internet of Things Into Software Engineering Practices* (pp. 125–145). Hershey, PA: IGI Global. doi:10.4018/978-1-5225-7790-4.ch006

Mansoor, M., Khan, M. W., Rizvi, S. S., Hashmani, M. A., & Zubair, M. (2019). Adaptation of Modern Agile Practices in Global Software Engineering. In M. Rehman, A. Amin, A. Gilal, & M. Hashmani (Eds.), *Human Factors in Global Software Engineering* (pp. 164–187). Hershey, PA: IGI Global. doi:10.4018/978-1-5225-9448-2.ch007

Memon, M. S. (2019). Techniques and Trends Towards Various Dimensions of Robust Security Testing in Global Software Engineering. In M. Rehman, A. Amin, A. Gilal, & M. Hashmani (Eds.), *Human Factors in Global Software Engineering* (pp. 219–251). Hershey, PA: IGI Global. doi:10.4018/978-1-5225-9448-2.ch009

Mookherjee, A., Mulay, P., Joshi, R., Prajapati, P. S., Johari, S., & Prajapati, S. S. (2019). Sentilyser: Embedding Voice Markers in Homeopathy Treatments. In A. Mukherjee & A. Krishna (Eds.), *Interdisciplinary Approaches to Information Systems and Software Engineering* (pp. 181–206). Hershey, PA: IGI Global. doi:10.4018/978-1-5225-7784-3.ch008

Mukherjee, S., Bhattacharjee, A. K., & Deyasi, A. (2019). Project Teamwork Assessment and Success Rate Prediction Through Meta-Heuristic Algorithms. In A. Mukherjee & A. Krishna (Eds.), *Interdisciplinary Approaches to Information Systems and Software Engineering* (pp. 33–61). Hershey, PA: IGI Global. doi:10.4018/978-1-5225-7784-3.ch003

Nandy, A. (2019). Identification of Tectonic Activity and Fault Mechanism From Morphological Signatures. In A. Mukherjee & A. Krishna (Eds.), *Interdisciplinary Approaches to Information Systems and Software Engineering* (pp. 99–123). Hershey, PA: IGI Global. doi:10.4018/978-1-5225-7784-3.ch005

Omar, M., Rejab, M. M., & Ahmad, M. (2019). The Effect of Team Work Quality on Team Performance in Global Software Engineering. In M. Rehman, A. Amin, A. Gilal, & M. Hashmani (Eds.), *Human Factors in Global Software Engineering* (pp. 322–331). Hershey, PA: IGI Global. doi:10.4018/978-1-5225-9448-2.ch013

Onuchowska, A., & de Vreede, G. (2017). Disruption and Deception in Crowdsourcing. *International Journal of e-Collaboration*, *13*(4), 23–41. doi:10.4018/IJeC.2017100102

Papadopoulou, C., & Giaoutzi, M. (2017). Crowdsourcing and Living Labs in Support of Smart Cities' Development. *International Journal of E-Planning Research*, *6*(2), 22–38. doi:10.4018/IJEPR.2017040102

Patnaik, K. S., & Snigdh, I. (2019). Modelling and Designing of IoT Systems Using UML Diagrams: An Introduction. In D. Mala (Ed.), *Integrating the Internet of Things Into Software Engineering Practices* (pp. 36–61). Hershey, PA: IGI Global. doi:10.4018/978-1-5225-7790-4.ch003

Pawar, L., Kumar, R., & Sharma, A. (2018). Risks Analysis and Mitigation Technique in EDA Sector: VLSI Supply Chain. In R. Kumar, A. Tayal, & S. Kapil (Eds.), *Analyzing the Role of Risk Mitigation and Monitoring in Software Development* (pp. 256–265). Hershey, PA: IGI Global. doi:10.4018/978-1-5225-6029-6.ch016

Persaud, A., & O'Brien, S. (2017). Quality and Acceptance of Crowdsourced Translation of Web Content. *International Journal of Technology and Human Interaction*, *13*(1), 100–115. doi:10.4018/IJTHI.2017010106

Phung, V. D., & Hawryszkiewycz, I. (2019). Knowledge Sharing and Innovative Work Behavior: An Extension of Social Cognitive Theory. In R. Lenart-Gansiniec (Ed.), *Crowdsourcing and Knowledge Management in Contemporary Business Environments* (pp. 71–102). Hershey, PA: IGI Global. doi:10.4018/978-1-5225-4200-1.ch005

Pohulak-Żołędowska, E. (2019). Crowdsourcing in Innovation Activity of Enterprises on an Example of Pharmaceutical Industry. In R. Lenart-Gansiniec (Ed.), *Crowdsourcing and Knowledge Management in Contemporary Business Environments* (pp. 58–70). Hershey, PA: IGI Global. doi:10.4018/978-1-5225-4200-1.ch004

Pramanik, P. K., Pal, S., Pareek, G., Dutta, S., & Choudhury, P. (2019). Crowd Computing: The Computing Revolution. In R. Lenart-Gansiniec (Ed.), *Crowdsourcing and Knowledge Management in Contemporary Business Environments* (pp. 166–198). Hershey, PA: IGI Global. doi:10.4018/978-1-5225-4200-1.ch009

Priakanth, P., & Gopikrishnan, S. (2019). Machine Learning Techniques for Internet of Things. In D. Mala (Ed.), *Integrating the Internet of Things Into Software Engineering Practices* (pp. 160–180). Hershey, PA: IGI Global. doi:10.4018/978-1-5225-7790-4.ch008

Priyadarshi, A. (2019). Segmentation of Different Tissues of Brain From MR Image. In A. Mukherjee & A. Krishna (Eds.), *Interdisciplinary Approaches to Information Systems and Software Engineering* (pp. 142–180). Hershey, PA: IGI Global. doi:10.4018/978-1-5225-7784-3.ch007

Rath, M. (2019). Intelligent Information System for Academic Institutions: Using Big Data Analytic Approach. In A. Mukherjee & A. Krishna (Eds.), *Interdisciplinary Approaches to Information Systems and Software Engineering* (pp. 207–232). Hershey, PA: IGI Global. doi:10.4018/978-1-5225-7784-3.ch009

Realyvásquez, A., Maldonado-Macías, A. A., & Hernández-Escobedo, G. (2019). Software Development for Ergonomic Compatibility Assessment of Advanced Manufacturing Technology. In M. Rehman, A. Amin, A. Gilal, & M. Hashmani (Eds.), *Human Factors in Global Software Engineering* (pp. 50–83). Hershey, PA: IGI Global. doi:10.4018/978-1-5225-9448-2.ch003

Saini, M., & Chahal, K. K. (2018). A Systematic Review of Attributes and Techniques for Open Source Software Evolution Analysis. In M. Khosrow-Pour, D.B.A. (Ed.), Optimizing Contemporary Application and Processes in Open Source Software (pp. 1-23). Hershey, PA: IGI Global. doi:10.4018/978-1-5225-5314-4.ch001

Sanga, C. A., Lyimo, N. N., Fue, K. G., Telemala, J. P., Kilima, F., & Kipanyula, M. J. (2019). Piloting Crowdsourcing Platform for Monitoring and Evaluation of Projects: Harnessing Massive Open Online Deliberation (MOOD). In R. Lenart-Gansiniec (Ed.), *Crowdsourcing and Knowledge Management in Contemporary Business Environments* (pp. 199–217). Hershey, PA: IGI Global. doi:10.4018/978-1-5225-4200-1.ch010

Sedkaoui, S. (2019). Data Analytics Supporting Knowledge Acquisition. In R. Lenart-Gansiniec (Ed.), *Crowdsourcing and Knowledge Management in Contemporary Business Environments* (pp. 146–165). Hershey, PA: IGI Global. doi:10.4018/978-1-5225-4200-1.ch008

Sen, K., & Ghosh, K. (2018). Designing Effective Crowdsourcing Systems for the Healthcare Industry. *International Journal of Public Health Management and Ethics*, *3*(2), 57–62. doi:10.4018/IJPHME.2018070104

Sen, K., & Ghosh, K. (2018). Incorporating Global Medical Knowledge to Solve Healthcare Problems: A Framework for a Crowdsourcing System. *International Journal of Healthcare Information Systems and Informatics*, *13*(1), 1–14. doi:10.4018/IJHISI.2018010101

Sharma, A., Pal, V., Ojha, N., & Bajaj, R. (2018). Risks Assessment in Designing Phase: Its Impacts and Issues. In R. Kumar, A. Tayal, & S. Kapil (Eds.), *Analyzing the Role of Risk Mitigation and Monitoring in Software Development* (pp. 46–60). Hershey, PA: IGI Global. doi:10.4018/978-1-5225-6029-6.ch004

Sharma, A., Pawar, L., & Kaur, M. (2018). Development and Enhancing of Software and Programming Products by Client Information Administration in Market. In R. Kumar, A. Tayal, & S. Kapil (Eds.), *Analyzing the Role of Risk Mitigation and Monitoring in Software Development* (pp. 150–187). Hershey, PA: IGI Global. doi:10.4018/978-1-5225-6029-6.ch010

Sharma, A. P., & Sharma, S. (2018). Risk Management in Web Development. In R. Kumar, A. Tayal, & S. Kapil (Eds.), *Analyzing the Role of Risk Mitigation and Monitoring in Software Development* (pp. 188–203). Hershey, PA: IGI Global. doi:10.4018/978-1-5225-6029-6.ch011

Sharma, I., & Chhabra, D. (2018). Meta-Heuristic Approach for Software Project Risk Schedule Analysis. In R. Kumar, A. Tayal, & S. Kapil (Eds.), *Analyzing the Role of Risk Mitigation and Monitoring in Software Development* (pp. 136–149). Hershey, PA: IGI Global. doi:10.4018/978-1-5225-6029-6.ch009

Sharma, S., & Dua, R. (2018). Gamification: An Effectual Learning Application for SE. In R. Kumar, A. Tayal, & S. Kapil (Eds.), *Analyzing the Role of Risk Mitigation and Monitoring in Software Development* (pp. 219–233). Hershey, PA: IGI Global. doi:10.4018/978-1-5225-6029-6.ch013

Shilohu Rao, N. J. P., Chaudhary, R. S., & Goswami, D. (2019). Knowledge Management System for Governance: Transformational Approach Creating Knowledge as Product for Governance. In R. Lenart-Gansiniec (Ed.), *Crowdsourcing and Knowledge Management in Contemporary Business Environments* (pp. 20–38). Hershey, PA: IGI Global. doi:10.4018/978-1-5225-4200-1.ch002

Sidhu, A. K., & Sehra, S. K. (2018). Use of Software Metrics to Improve the Quality of Software Projects Using Regression Testing. In R. Kumar, A. Tayal, & S. Kapil (Eds.), *Analyzing the Role of Risk Mitigation and Monitoring in Software Development* (pp. 204–218). Hershey, PA: IGI Global. doi:10.4018/978-1-5225-6029-6.ch012

Srao, B. K., Rai, H. S., & Mann, K. S. (2018). Why India Should Make It Compulsory to Go for BIM. In R. Kumar, A. Tayal, & S. Kapil (Eds.), *Analyzing the Role of Risk Mitigation and Monitoring in Software Development* (pp. 266–277). Hershey, PA: IGI Global. doi:10.4018/978-1-5225-6029-6.ch017

Srivastava, R. (2018). An Analysis on Risk Management and Risk in the Software Projects. In R. Kumar, A. Tayal, & S. Kapil (Eds.), *Analyzing the Role of Risk Mitigation and Monitoring in Software Development* (pp. 83–99). Hershey, PA: IGI Global. doi:10.4018/978-1-5225-6029-6.ch006

Srivastava, R., Verma, S. K., & Thukral, V. (2018). A New Approach for Reinforcement of Project DEMATEL-FMCDM-TODIM Fuzzy Approach. In R. Kumar, A. Tayal, & S. Kapil (Eds.), *Analyzing the Role of Risk Mitigation and Monitoring in Software Development* (pp. 234–243). Hershey, PA: IGI Global. doi:10.4018/978-1-5225-6029-6.ch014

Tolu, H. (2018). Strategy of Good Software Governance: FLOSS in the State of Turkey. In M. Khosrow-Pour, D.B.A. (Ed.), Optimizing Contemporary Application and Processes in Open Source Software (pp. 198-221). Hershey, PA: IGI Global. doi:10.4018/978-1-5225-5314-4.ch008

Trad, A. (2019). The Business Transformation Framework and Enterprise Architecture Framework for Managers in Business Innovation: Knowledge Management in Global Software Engineering (KMGSE). In M. Rehman, A. Amin, A. Gilal, & M. Hashmani (Eds.), *Human Factors in Global Software Engineering* (pp. 20–49). Hershey, PA: IGI Global. doi:10.4018/978-1-5225-9448-2.ch002

Vasanthapriyan, S. (2019). Knowledge Management Initiatives in Agile Software Development: A Literature Review. In M. Rehman, A. Amin, A. Gilal, & M. Hashmani (Eds.), *Human Factors in Global Software Engineering* (pp. 109–130). Hershey, PA: IGI Global. doi:10.4018/978-1-5225-9448-2.ch005

Vasanthapriyan, S. (2019). Knowledge Sharing Initiatives in Software Companies: A Mapping Study. In M. Rehman, A. Amin, A. Gilal, & M. Hashmani (Eds.), *Human Factors in Global Software Engineering* (pp. 84–108). Hershey, PA: IGI Global. doi:10.4018/978-1-5225-9448-2.ch004

Vasanthapriyan, S. (2019). Study of Employee Innovative Behavior in Sri Lankan Software Companies. In M. Rehman, A. Amin, A. Gilal, & M. Hashmani (Eds.), *Human Factors in Global Software Engineering* (pp. 188–218). Hershey, PA: IGI Global. doi:10.4018/978-1-5225-9448-2.ch008

Zaei, M. E. (2019). Knowledge Management in the Non-Governmental Organizations Context. In R. Lenart-Gansiniec (Ed.), *Crowdsourcing and Knowledge Management in Contemporary Business Environments* (pp. 39–57). Hershey, PA: IGI Global. doi:10.4018/978-1-5225-4200-1.ch003

Ziouvelou, X., & McGroarty, F. (2018). A Business Model Framework for Crowd-Driven IoT Ecosystems. *International Journal of Social Ecology and Sustainable Development, 9*(3), 14–33. doi:10.4018/IJSESD.2018070102

Zykov, S. V., Gromoff, A., & Kazantsev, N. S. (2019). *Software Engineering for Enterprise System Agility: Emerging Research and Opportunities* (pp. 1–218). Hershey, PA: IGI Global. doi:10.4018/978-1-5225-5589-6

About the Contributors

Varun Gupta received his Ph.D & Master of Technology (By Research) in Computer Science & Engineering from Uttarakhand Technical University and Bachelor of Technology (Hon's) from Himachal Pradesh University respectively. Dr. Varun Gupta is working with Universidade da Beira Interior, Portugal. He is also Honorary Research Fellow of the University of Salford, Manchester, United Kingdom. He is Associate Editor of IEEE Access (Published by IEEE, SCIE Indexed with 4.098 impact factor), Associate Editor of International Journal of Computer Aided Engineering & Technology (Published by Inderscience Publishers, Scopus indexed), Associate Editor of IEEE Software Blog, Associate editor of Journal of Cases on Information Technology (JCIT) (Published by IGI Global and Indexed by Emerging Sources Citation Index (ESCI) & SCOPUS) and former Editorial Team Member of British Journal of Educational Technology (BJET) (Published by Wiley publishers, SCIE Indexed with 2.729 impact factor). He had been Guest Editor of many special issues published/ongoing with leading International Journals and Editor of many edited books to be published by IGI Global and Taylor & Francis (CRC Press). He had organised many special session with Scopus Indexed International Conferences world wide, proceedings of which were published by Springer, IEEE, Elsevier etc. He is serving as reviewer of IEEE Transactions on Emerging Topics in Computational Intelligence. He had guided One Doctoral (Ph.D.), Four Masters (M.Tech) and 52 Bachelor (B.Tech.) Projects in interdisciplinary areas. His area of interest is Evolutionary Software Engineering (focusing on Requirement management, Global developments, Software Testing) for multinational firms and Start-ups.

* * *

Utkarsh Agrawal completed his B. Tech. in Computer Science from Amity University in Noida, Uttar Pradesh, India.

Priyanka Chandani is a Research Scholar at Jaypee Institute of Information Technology, India. She is currently pursuing her Ph.D from the same. She also holds a Masters of Technology and a Bachelor of Technology degree in Information Technology. She has also worked in Infosys Technologies and TechMahindra. Her research interest includes Software Quality, Software Testing and Requirements Engineering.

D. S. Chauhan is the Vice Chancellor of GLA University Mathura, President AIU, New Delhi, India.

Dhanaselvi D. is a Project Engineer (IV&V) with Aeronautical Development Agency, Bangalore, Ministry of Defence, Government of India.

Zayaraz Godandapani is currently working as Professor in the Department of Computer Science and Engineering, Pondicherry Engineering College. His areas of interests include Software Engineering and Information Security. He completed his B.Tech., M.Tech. and PhD in computer Science and engineering from Pondicherry University. He has 28 years of teaching experience at all levels namely industry, diploma, under graduate, post graduate and research. He has officiated as Head of MCA department and currently is the Associate Dean (Student Affairs). To his credit he has published more than hundred research papers in reputed International Journals and Conferences. He has authored a book titled Quantitative Evaluation of Software Architectures sold by leading book sellers. He has been the advisory member, and reviewer for several International Conferences. He has been the Guest editor of Inderscience special issue journal on software engineering. Under his guidance, 7 Scholars have successfully completed their PhD and 4 students are pursuing their PhD.

Chetna Gupta is Associate Professor at Jaypee Institute of Information Technology, Noida, India. She holds Ph.D, Masters of Technology and a Bachelor of Engineering degree in Computer Science and Engineering. Her area of research is software engineering - requirement engineering, software testing, software project management and data mining, with emphasis on software testing, software re-usability and analysis. Her research to date has involved program analysis to compute and provide the kinds of analysis information about a program, such as data-flow, change impact sets, classification of data using software engineering concepts and data mining, predicting software components for reuse - needed for software engineering tasks for estimating impact analysis, regression testing.

Shruti Gupta is working as Assistant Professor in Amity University in the dept of Computer science and Engineering. My interest is to provide the best result to serve the mankind and by taking care of environment.

Astha Kumari is a Final year B.Tech student of Department of CSE/IT at Jaypee Institute of Information Technology.

Vimaladevi M is currently a research scholar in the Department of Computer Science and Engineering, Pondicherry Engineering College. She completed her B.Tech. and M.Tech. in Computer Science and Engineering from Pondicherry University. She has 13 years of work experience in both industry and academics. She had been working as Project Lead in L&T Infotech for Hitachi client. She had executed various projects and involved in all the phases of software life cycle including planning and estimation, design, development and testing. She is experienced in executing projects in various process models like Waterfall, V-model and Agile. She was involved in the quality analysis and assessment of the software, client communication and received customer appreciation. Her areas of interest include software Engineering, Project Estimation and Project management and Process Models.

Kamalendu Pal is with the Department of Computer Science, School of Mathematics, Computer Science and Engineering, City, University London. Kamalendu received his BSc (Hons) degree in Physics from Calcutta University, India, Postgraduate Diploma in Computer Science from Pune, India; MSc degree in Software Systems Technology from Sheffield University, Postgraduate Diploma in Artificial Intelligence from Kingston University, MPhil degree in Computer Science from University College London, and MBA degree from University of Hull, United Kingdom. He has published dozens of research papers in international journals and conferences. His research interests include knowledge-based systems, decision support systems, computer integrated design, software engineering, and service-oriented computing. He is a member of the British Computer Society, the Institution of Engineering and Technology, and the IEEE Computer Society.

Rekha R. is a scientist and Technology Director (IV&V) with Aeronautical Development Agency, Bangalore, Ministry of Defence, Government of India.

Surbhi Singhal is a Final year B.Tech student of Department of CSE/IT at Jaypee Institute of Information Technology.

Sudha Srinivasan is a scientist with Aeronautical Development Agency, Bangalore, Ministry of Defence, Government of India. She has over 20 years of experience in the field of software engineering.

Srinivasan Vaidyanathan has been an accomplished and results-driven delivery director in IT industry and has over 24 years of progressive, managerial and leadership experience in high visibility and multifaceted roles in IT majors, Cognizant and Capgemini. He had led large-scale software deliveries for several flagship customers that cut across industrial sectors. He has demonstrated success of delivery management, business development, Resource Planning, Financials, HR and Quality Management in his professional domain. He has hands-on experience in leading Knowledge Management at various capacities of his corporate tenure. He has proven abilities to implement standards, procedures, and processes that improve software delivery quality. He has a PhD in Management and his PhD thesis is in the area of Knowledge Sharing and Creation through Social Media. He has published book chapters and research papers in reputed journals and publications.

Index

A

Airborne Embedded Systems 35-36, 38, 46, 48-49, 153, 161
aircraft subsystems 35-36, 40, 43
Anti-fragility 109, 119, 125

C

Cloud computing 23, 33
Code Smells 132
Computing and Decision Making 94, 146
Construction Management 94, 146-147
Crowdsourcing 1-7, 19-22, 120, 126
Crowdsourcing Software Engineering 22

D

data mining 23, 31
Decision Making 4, 7, 24, 27, 32, 63, 75, 77, 80, 83, 92, 94, 114, 146
DO-254 154-155, 161, 163, 165-166

E

Extreme programming 81-86, 88, 90-93

F

Fault Injection 119, 131-132
Field Programmable Gate Arrays (FPGA) 153-154
Financial Estimation 146

G

global software development 81-82, 90, 92

H

Human Computer Interaction 134
Human Intelligence Tasks 1-2, 4, 22

I

Impact Analysis 42, 44

K

knowledge extraction 23, 28

M

machine learning 23, 25, 29, 56, 62, 75
Markov Decision Theory 1, 21-22
module level testing 35, 38-41, 46, 48
Multi-Objective Optimization 122, 132

N

Non-Functional Requirement 132

P

practitioners 5, 24, 61, 81-83, 87-90, 92

Q

Quality Attributes 62, 76, 109, 111-112, 115, 117, 121-123, 127, 129

R

Refactoring 86, 109, 112, 121-131
regular expressions 42-43
requirement based testing 35-38, 42, 45, 47-48
requirement engineering 51, 53, 56, 67, 69-70, 77
requirement reuse 23-24, 26
Risk Assessment 52-57, 61-63, 66, 68-69, 71-73, 75-79
Risk Management 51-53, 56, 62, 66-80, 93, 117

S

Scenario-Based Evaluation 132
Search Based Software Engineering 123
Software Ageing 132
Software Architecture Evaluation 127, 131

Software Development 1, 3-4, 6-8, 14, 20, 22, 35-39, 47, 50-52, 56, 61-63, 67, 69, 71-74, 77, 79, 81-85, 90-93, 110-111, 114, 117-118, 120, 125-126, 128-129, 161
Software Metrics 62-63, 72, 115-116, 123, 126, 129, 132
Software Process Model 1, 3, 22
Software Process Modelling 21
Software Prototyping 134
Software Resilience 128
Software Structural Characteristics 133
software system testing 36, 38, 40-42
structural coverage 38, 40, 45-46

T

test planning 35, 38

U

User Interface Designing 134-135, 138

Ensure Quality Research is Introduced to the Academic Community

Become an IGI Global Reviewer for Authored Book Projects

The overall success of an authored book project is dependent on quality and timely reviews.

In this competitive age of scholarly publishing, constructive and timely feedback significantly expedites the turnaround time of manuscripts from submission to acceptance, allowing the publication and discovery of forward-thinking research at a much more expeditious rate. Several IGI Global authored book projects are currently seeking highly-qualified experts in the field to fill vacancies on their respective editorial review boards:

Applications and Inquiries may be sent to:
development@igi-global.com

Applicants must have a doctorate (or an equivalent degree) as well as publishing and reviewing experience. Reviewers are asked to complete the open-ended evaluation questions with as much detail as possible in a timely, collegial, and constructive manner. All reviewers' tenures run for one-year terms on the editorial review boards and are expected to complete at least three reviews per term. Upon successful completion of this term, reviewers can be considered for an additional term.

If you have a colleague that may be interested in this opportunity, we encourage you to share this information with them.

IGI Global Proudly Partners With eContent Pro International

Receive a 25% Discount on all Editorial Services

Editorial Services

IGI Global expects all final manuscripts submitted for publication to be in their final form. This means they must be reviewed, revised, and professionally copy edited prior to their final submission. Not only does this support with accelerating the publication process, but it also ensures that the highest quality scholarly work can be disseminated.

English Language Copy Editing

Let eContent Pro International's expert copy editors perform edits on your manuscript to resolve spelling, punctuaion, grammar, syntax, flow, formatting issues and more.

Scientific and Scholarly Editing

Allow colleagues in your research area to examine the content of your manuscript and provide you with valuable feedback and suggestions before submission.

Figure, Table, Chart & Equation Conversions

Do you have poor quality figures? Do you need visual elements in your manuscript created or converted? A design expert can help!

Translation

Need your documjent translated into English? eContent Pro International's expert translators are fluent in English and more than 40 different languages.

Email: customerservice@econtentpro.com   **www.igi-global.com/editorial-service-partners**

Printed in the United States
By Bookmasters